California Rancho Cooking

Jacqueline Higuera Mc Mahan

Book Design by Robert McMahan

THE OLIVE PRESS

Requests for permission to make copies of any part
of the work should be mailed to:
The Olive Press, P.O. Box 194, Lake Hughes, Ca. 93532.

Book Design: Robert McMahan
Engravings: R. Bulman

LIBRARY OF CONGRESS CATALOGING IN PUBLICATION
McMahan, Jacqueline
California rancho cooking.
Includes index.
1.   Cookery, California.   2.   Rancho, California
Landgrant History   I.   Title.
Catalog Card No. 83-72309
ISBN 0-9612150-7-0

THIRD PRINTING, SEPTEMBER 1988

Printed in the United States of America

*"And I brought you into a plentiful country,
to eat the fruit thereof, and the goodness thereof..."*
Mission father to Spanish settlers of Alta California
at end of the 18th century

Grandmama as a young woman, at the turn of the twentieth century.

To Grandmama and Mama,
who taught me first to love
the ceremony of eating,
and then gave me their kitchens.

CONTENTS

ACKNOWLEDGMENTS

The accomplishment of a book requires a great deal of re-search, persistence, and believers in the task at hand.

To my husband Robert goes my deepest gratitude for giving me his faith and always loving the magic of ancient olive groves especially when a picnic is provided. He worked hard, tasted, cajoled, got angry at the right times, and refused to ever let me retreat.

To Robert's mother and my friend, Mabel M. McMahan, who believed far beyond the role model set by most mothers-in-law.

To Elizabeth Ann Johnson for her excitement over rancho California cooking and a belief that it is one of our great regional cuisines.

To Chris Duncan Leppert who believes in this book almost as much as she loves chile and chiles. Chris' hours and hours at a typewriter produced an accurate manuscript and she never got angry, in front of me, for making "just one more change" in the copy as recipes were retested.

To Stephanie Ratzburg for her valuable historical research.

To the late Father Maynard Geiger, Santa Barbara Mission Archives for opening the mission doors and loaning me precious books.

To the long line of Higuera, Silva, and Chavarria cooks, and friends who contributed their ideas and favorite recipes throughout the years.

To my sons, Ian and O'Reilly who always try to have the last word in the kitchen.

The original United States government map showing the official boundaries of the Higuera land grant rancho.

"El que no arriesga no pasa el mar."   He who doesn't take a chance never crosses the ocean.   Old Spanish proverb.

1775   Ygnacio Higuera, my great-great-great grandfather came up with the fabled Anza party, on the overland route, from Mexico to Monterey, California. Their goal was to bring more settlers to colonize Spain's Pacific frontier, thereby protecting California from the infringement of covetous nations. Ygnacio a young *soldado de cuera*, found romance and was married along the way to Maria Bojorques who was traveling with her family. Later, Ygnacio became a majordomo of the Pueblo San Jose and was tragically killed by Indians in 1805 while accompanying a mission priest on a trek into the wilderness.

1821   Ygnacio's son, Jose Loreto Higuera, was issued one of the last of Spain's royal land grants, before Mexico made its claim upon California and declared independence from Spain. The land grant, 4,394 acres, was on the eastern side of San Francisco Bay, skirting the lush foothills of the Diablo mountains. It was named Rancho Los Tularcitos.

1828	The family's main house, a large rectangular adobe, was constructed to shelter the huge family - nineteen children from three marriages. The legendary olive grove was planted by Don José and the road that wound its way through the double row of trees, known as The Lane, became the symbol of Los Tularcitos and the source of many tales.
1835-45	The Rancho was frequently marauded by Indians. Don Valentín, elder son of Don José, joined other rancheros and successfully pursued Indians who had stolen 600 of their horses.
1839	Renewal of the title to Los Tularcitos, under the laws of Mexico.
1840	María Higuera, my great-grandmother, was born and became one of Don Valentín's favorite daughters. Later, when she married Nicolas Chavarria, a Chilean, she was given a dowry of land along with a lavish wedding that lasted for days and days.
1845	As a result of a fatal fall from his spirited horse, Don José died at the age of 67 and his most able son, Don Valentín, became the patriarch of the large family. He operated the ranch lucratively, running a mill on the ranch property, selling grain to the Russians in Sacramento during the Gold

Rush and raising cattle, but as the Americanization of California came about he began to lose his stake in the land. The least of his troubles were his twelve children and the eighteen offspring of his father, the virile Don José Loreto; everyone required a piece of the land.

1867   Frank Chavarria, my grandfather, was born to María Higuera Chavarria. Don Valentín was still alive, a living legend of the days when the rancho had been productive. Land had slowly disappeared in portions by suspicious dealings, numerous dowries, and because of the Californios' poor business sense, otherwise known as Spanish honor: Where money was concerned they did not feel it honorable to fight. Through tales passed down in the family, the loss of land was blamed on gambling, María Higuera's huge wedding and the high cost of fandangos. Actually, a major portion of Los Tularcitos was sold to a Frenchman by the name of Columbet whose farcical scheme to turn the main ranch house into a luxury hotel and gambling casino failed and he then sold the land to Henry Curtner.

1870   Patent issued by the United States government for the Rancho Los Tularcitos, half of which was already gone.

1900   The Higuera family continued to live on the wedding gift of land given to Maria and Nicolas; and land which Nicolas had acquired himself was planted with fruit orchards. Much of the 4,394 acres was gone, but they lived contentedly still entertaining with lavish barbeques as though these were still the golden days.

1947   The remains of Los Tularcitos and the last of the wedding dowry of María and Nicolas was sold for a pittance when my grandfather quarreled with one of his brothers over some proceeds from the walnut orchards.

NOW   The Los Tularcitos adobe, now restored, is part of a city park. The Lane still stands after a heated battle to preserve the old olive trees whose proximity to the freeway was considered a nuisance. The Lane is deep with neglected leaves and the knarled trees cross their branches above creating a natural archway - within their protection it is hushed except for the muffled sound of speeding cars.

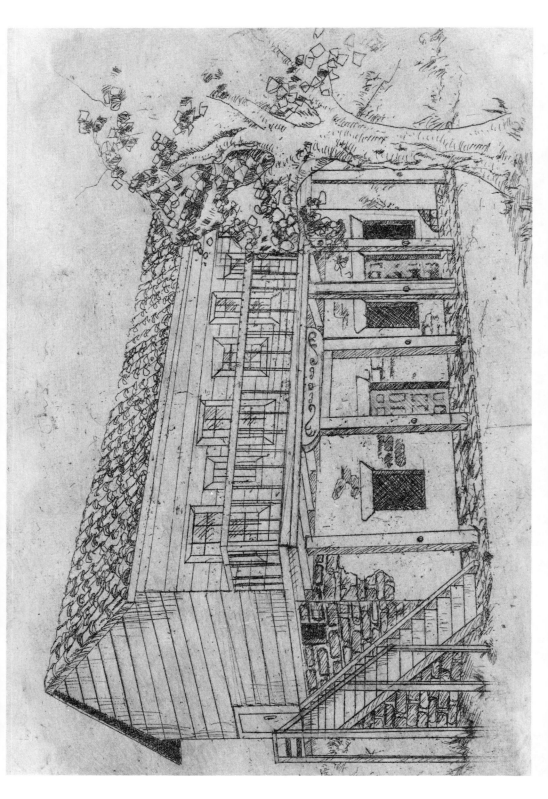

The original adobe of Jose Loreto Higuera with the second floor addition.

CHAPTER I

THE RANCHO

The Early Days to the Present

lta California, as the land of the mythical god-
dess, Califia, was known in earlier days, was a
country in itself, surrounded by wilderness and an
ocean to the west. Travelers had to submit to
many hardships before reaching this place and, in the beginning,
life for its Spanish settlers was neither prosperous nor civilized.
The Californio was alone in paradise, amongst his paisanos and
a few mission priests. The spoken tongue was Spanish and was
considered, by those speaking it, to be the language of God.
English, only spoken by foreigners, seemed rough to the ear and
was deemed the idiom of birds. The Californios were convinced
they were living in the grace of God. For a while, perhaps they
were.

In 1821 the last Spanish governor of Alta California, Pablo Vicente de Sola, granted to my great-great-great grandfather, Don Jose Loreto Higuera, 4,394 acres of the fertile soil skirting the Santa Clara valley, known earlier as the Llano de Los Robles, a lush plain covered with noble oaks and blue lupine, golden poppies, and mustard in the springtime. Wild oats grew so high horsemen could tie the grasses together above their horses' saddles.

The rancho was self-sufficient by the mid-nineteenth century and, with its *gente de razón* and indios, was reminiscent of feudal times. The rhythm of life was set by the Don, who arose with the lucero, the morning star. After prayer and a cup of hot chocolate, he rode off with his vaqueros to check the cattle. He lived on horseback until he died. The hours of the day were kept by the return of the riders for meals.

Around mid-morning, almuerzo would be served - a breakfast of chorizo sausage, fried and accompanied by eggs or mixed with frijoles. There would be refried beans shaped into a thin pancake, a stack of flour tortillas, some red wine, fruit and perhaps coffee made with burnt wheat if coffee beans had not come on the last ship from Mexico. When they were inside the adobe ranch house, doors were left open as if they did not exist and ladies sat in the thick window ledges, shutters thrown open, looking out as the backs of the riders disappeared again into the hills to keep watch over the cattle - or just to ride for the pure joy of riding.

IN THE MEMORIES OF A CHILD'S EYES, I SEE THE LANE, THE LONG OLIVE GROVE SILVERY GREEN, KEEPING OUT THE SUN, LEADING TO A RAMBLING RANCHHOUSE, SURROUNDED BY GNARLED FIG TREES AND EVERYWHERE, CRUMBLING ADOBE WALLS AND BUILDINGS, GHOSTLY REMINDERS.

In this idyllic land where few silver coins passed from hand to hand, business affairs were bound by gentlemen's agreements, a glass of wine and an abrazo. The Californios carried on a sixteenth century pastoral existence in the nineteenth century. The hides from cattle, spoken of as California money, were traded for any of the luxuries thought necessary to life such as chocolate, a silk shawl from China, or a new pair of boots. In 1830 money was still scarcely part of the value system, a fact that later brought about the tragic undoing of many a rancho family, including my own. A bowl of silver coins was customarily left in the room of a guest, to take from as was needed for the journey ahead. When too many visiting Americans took the whole bowl, the old custom could no longer be observed.

WHEAT WAS GROWN WITH MUCH LESS EFFORT THAN CORN, WHICH NEEDED IRRIGATION. WHEAT FLOUR TORTILLAS BECAME THE EARLY BREAD OF CALIFORNIA RATHER THAN THE TORTILLAS DE MAÍZ KNOWN TO MEXICO. TO GRANDMAMA, THE SUBJECT WAS CLOSED. GENTLE FOLK ATE THE FLOUR TORTILLAS THAT WOULD UNFOLD LIKE THE PETALS OF A FLOWER FROM THE BASKET LINED WITH A WHITE NAPKIN.

Irregularly, sailing ships from around the Horn would come bearing *gran pipas* filled with coffee beans, wine, chocolate, sugar and other extravagances which could not be had on what Richard Henry Dana called a "half-civilized coast." This young Bostonian was highly perturbed at being fed a constant diet of beans although he did admit to the California bean being the best in the world, when well-cooked. In this isolated land, foreigners protested at the primitiveness of food and lodging but the Californios were happy to have paradise to themselves, with no great need for money or hard work and time to sit down to a simple but plentiful table with children and friends.

IN THE BEGINNING OF THE EARLY NINETEENTH CENTURY THE FOODS EATEN ON THE RANCHO WERE PARTLY INDIAN, PARTLY MEXICAN AND PARTLY FOOD CREATED FROM A WILDERNESS. WHEN I WAS A CHILD, IN THE 1940'S, MY BLIND AUNT NICOLASSA WOULD HAVE ME LEAD HER AROUND THE PRICKLY CACTUS HEDGES THAT WERE ONCE THE FORBIDDING FENCES OF THE RANCHO, AND TAKE HER TO THE FIELD ACROSS CALERA CREEK WHERE WE WOULD GATHER THE TINY HORSEBEANS GROWING THERE. IN THE EARLY SPRING, GRANDMAMA AND I WOULD SPEND A WHOLE AFTERNOON WITH OUR BASKETS, SEARCHING FOR THE SMALLEST AND MOST TENDER LEAVES GROWING ON THE WILD MUSTARD PLANTS. MOSTAZA HAD BEEN EATEN BY OUR FORBEARS ONE HUNDRED FIFTY YEARS BEFORE WHEN THEY WERE HUNGRY FOR SOMETHING GREEN AND THE ONLY CULTIVATED GARDENS WERE THOSE OWNED BY THE MISSIONS. BY THE CREEKBED ALONGSIDE THE OLDEST HIGUERA ADOBE WE WOULD PICK STINGING NETTLES IF WE COULD FIND THE OLD GLOVES TO PROTECT OUR HANDS AND AUNT NICOLASSA WOULD STEAM THEM, MINCE THEM FINELY AND MIX THEM WITH CREAM. NOW WHEN I FIX THESE WILD THINGS FOR MY CHILDREN WE ENJOY THEM SMUGLY, AS IF WE WERE EATING LOST TREASURES. AND WE ARE.

On Rancho Los Tularcitos, they were famous for their *frijoles de olla*, always gloriously well-cooked and eaten zealously with every meal. The frijol to them was as pasta to the Italians. The huge midday meal on the ranch always brought *frijoles de olla*, *frijoles refritos*, a puchero or stew, carne con chile, flour tortillas, fruit and coffee. Sugar was scarce so desserts were rare, but with civilization came sweets.

By the 1860's, even with the crush of change, the social life on the ranchos continued with the fandangos, wakes, weddings and picnics. But it seemed as though they were celebrating in the midst of coming disaster. Many land grant ranchos were lost or greatly diminished in the years that followed the gold rush and the inevitable land rush. Californios were swept up by the new order. By the end of the nineteenth century, they were in the minority and the paradise they had known was gone.

ON THE DWINDLING RANCHO LOS TULARCITOS, LIFE STILL WENT ON -- CLINGING TO THE OLD STYLE. THERE IS AN OLD SPANISH SAYING: "NO HAPPINESS CAN COME TO A MAN WHO COMES BY MONEY TOO EASILY OR TO ONE WHO SEARCHES FOR TREASURE." SO IT SEEMED BEST TO LET THE WORLD SLIP BY WHILE YOU SAT IN THE GRAPE ARBOR WITH YOUR CHILDREN AND COMPADRES, TELLING STORIES PAST DUSK, RECOUNTING THE DAYS THAT GREW BETTER WITH THE TELLING. GRANDPA WOULD CALL FOR A BOWL OF APPLES AND WITH HIS POCKET KNIFE PEEL AN APPLE FOR EACH CHILD, THE PEEL UNFOLDING IN A LONG SPIRAL AS HE TALKED. FINALLY, HE WOULD TAKE US INSIDE THE RANCHHOUSE - WITH STILL NO ELECTRICITY IN THE MID-TWENTIETH CEN-

TURY - THE KEROSENE LIGHTS MAKING SHADOWS ON THE WALLS. HE HAD NAMES FOR THE SHADOWS - IGNACIO, JOAQUIN, VALENTIN - THE NAMES OF THE PAST THAT HE WANTED US TO REMEMBER. HE WOULD SAY IN A WHISPER, "CAN YOU HEAR THE VOICES COMING DOWN THE LANE?" HE NEVER FAILED TO ASK. IT WAS ALL PART OF A STORY THAT ENDED LONG AGO.

THE GREAT RANCHO WAS GONE, THE LEAGUES OF LAND DIMINISHED. WE PLAYED HIDE AND SEEK AMONGST THE RUINS OF OLD ADOBES AND IN THE BOWER OF THE ROOTED BRANCHES OF A CENTURY OLD FIG TREE WHERE NEW TREES HAD GROWN AROUND THE OLD TO CREATE A DOME. I LOVED TO SIT BEHIND AN OLD WALL AND LISTEN TO THE HUM OF THE CICADAS UNTIL AUNT NICOLASSA, SIGHTLESS, WOULD COME CALLING FOR ME - EXACTLY TO THE SPOT WHERE I WAS HIDING.

Long before the turn of the twentieth century, the great days of the California rancho had ended. Grandpa's stories touched the past for us, and we speak of it now to our children as something they will never know for they have never hidden amongst ruins on a quiet afternoon. And we have taken our children into The Lane, the long grove of olive trees planted in 1830, quieted them as we stood on the mulch of twenty years' carpet of leaves, and told them to listen, as Grandpa told us. And if you listen, there is more than the breeze and the distant sound of a freeway.

AS A CHILD, I LOOKED FORWARD TO STAYING WITH GRANDMAMA AND GRANDPA FOR I KNEW WHEN EVENING CAME THERE WOULD BE MERIENDA, THE TRADITION OF HOT CHOCOLATE, SWEET ROLLS,

6

BREAD AND JAM, AND CAKES SPREAD OUT OVER SNOWY LINEN. I WOULD EAT VERY SLOWLY, SIP-PING, AND CHOOSING FROM EACH JEWEL LAID BE-FORE ME. YEARS LATER, WHEN GRANDMAMA WAS NINETY AND HAD DECIDED SHE WAS GOING TO DIE, SHE GAVE ME ALL OF HER TABLECLOTHS. ONLY THEN DID I REALIZE THE LINENS AND FINE LACES I REMEMBERED ON HER TABLE WERE PLAIN COTTON UNDER HER SPELL. BUT THE FOOD, SOMETIMES JUST WARM AND COMFORTING, SOMETIMES EXOTIC AND RICH, HAD ALWAYS BEEN THERE.

"EL QUE CANTA, SU MAL ESPANTA." HE WHO SINGS, FRIGHTENS AWAY HIS ILL FORTUNE. AND ON THE RANCH, EATING WAS A WAY OF SINGING.

Grandpa tending to the fires in his asador's costume.

CHAPTER II

THE TRADITION OF BARBEQUES

n the twentieth century Rancho Los Tularcitos was no longer a hacienda bustling with vaqueros, Indian helpers and a great house full of children. On the few remaining acres life continued. The family found a comfortable existence on the semblance of what once was. My great-uncles who oversaw the land remained bachelors, growing old and bent as the one hundred year old pear trees growing along Calera Creek. The trees still gave promise of fruit every year and the uncles tended to the fruit.

And then came the weekends, bringing throngs of guests to the ranch – the brothers from town with their wives and children, the numerous friends and cousins, the Higuera relatives from Oakland, and on occasion a few dignitaries from San Francisco or San Jose. Grandmama and Grandpa, the chief asador, came every Saturday, with their five children in tow, to supervise the barbeques. The quiet old adobe, a century old, resounded with happy voices - women preparing foods, the men chatting with glasses in hand, and children everywhere.

It was never easy for children to sleep in the adobe ranch house haunted by spirits that stirred throughout the long nights and, as if that was not enough, the coyotes came down from the foothills and howled in the moonlight. On each bed, with their mattresses of sheep's wool, were three children huddled together listening to the ghosts prowling in the parlor, the room where all the wakes had been held in earlier days.

One night Mama's brothers, Edward and William, decided to prowl around too. They put their heads up to one of the ancient walls only to have their half-belief in ghosts confirmed. Coming from inside the wall were voices mumbling in Spanish. They grabbed one another and ran back to bed awakening all the other children with their cries about ghosts. They all sat up in bed until morning. Many days later, when they could no longer stand the teasing of their uncles, they got up the courage to listen to the old wall in the comfort of broad daylight. The more they listened the redder their faces turned, for the wall was the home of a swarm of bees, Spanish bees perhaps.

Many a Saturday night was survived in the haunted ranch house with tired children awakening to the sound of preparations for the barbeque. The women would be stretching flour tortillas and assembling the huge, red enchiladas filled with cheese, onions and black olives. Fresh watermelons would be

9

picked for dessert, along with any other fresh fruit ripening in the orchards. Early in the morning someone would be sent to collect palm fronds for a makeshift broom so the pathways and gardens could be swept before guests arrived.

The fires of oak and walnut were started four hours in advance, in a shallow pit later covered with grills or parillas. Most of the time, whole beef roasts were rubbed with a dry marinade of herbs and garlic and then placed in stoneware crocks days before the barbeque. For special occasions, an ox or bull's head was cooked in a stone-lined pit. Legs of lamb were roasted on a spit as Bapa basted with wine and garlic using long branches of green oregano. Just before removing the meat he tossed in the branches of green oregano for a last puff of herbal essence.

On barbeque day Bapa dressed in his fresh white asador's suit and the chef's toque and, thus attired, surveyed the preparation of the fires in the morning. When the fires had burned down to whitened coals, he attended to the cooking with great relish. For me, Bapa will always be the model of the exemplary asador. He would have been horrified at the modern concept of barbequing with charcoal briquets, starter fluids and bottled sauces; the cook who throws steaks on the grill to return twenty minutes later to check on them deserves a purgatory of burnt steaks. With wine glass in hand, Bapa constantly checked his fires.

Near the grill there was always a big coffee can filled with water and a long stick with a rag tied on the end. If the fire suddenly leaped into flames, the rag was dipped into the water and dribbled over the hot spot. I remember the barbeque taking a very long time and people wandering over and trying to cut off pieces of meat. Grandpa would playfully chase them off with his long fork. But I would wait until what I knew to be the right time, then go stand quietly by his side. And he, just as quietly, would take out some crusty bread (he always had the bread tucked away somewhere) and there would proceed my favorite part of the barbeque - he would tear off the bread and dab at the juices of the grilling meat. To go with the marvelous, black, smoky-oregano-tasting bread were the snippets of meat he cut off with his pocket knife. I knew with all the wisdom of a six-year old that I should be discreet about our tasting ritual.

During the long hours of barbequing there was much merrymaking, sipping of wine and wandering amidst the orchards and grounds. Carrying their glasses, the ladies in their dresses and the men in their suits walked about the trees or up to the foothills to look at the view of San Francisco Bay, toward Milpitas, the closest little town. In the later days of the ranch, the bowler hats and suits gave way to more comfortable attire for country life.

Another favorite spot to go was the old cactus hedge which had served as a fence for the hacienda in the last century when marauders and Indians were a real danger. The children knocked down the ripe prickly pears, or tunas, from the cactus and impaled the fruit on the end of a twig that had been whittled to a sharp point. Still holding the pear on the stick the

11

children used the large thistles of the nearby artichoke plant to brush off the painfully sharp spines of the prickly pear. The skin was peeled down, like the petals of a flower, revealing the shocking pink fruit inside. Eaten this way, standing in a thicket or some other wild place, a prickly pear tastes its best. They were never brought home to eat in a dish, civilized fashion.

Around midday, after everyone had wandered and played, the meat that had been so carefully tended, was brought to the table by Grandpa. The long tables, covered with white cloths, were laden with salads, enchiladas, sarsa, stacks of tortillas and great platters of the barbequed meats. With ravenous appetites everyone sat down to the outdoor feast, near their beloved trees and grape arbor. No one could imagine eating inside a dining room and, besides, there would not be enough room for all the guests and the numerous children.

Glasses were lifted to many toasts: To the food. To the day. To the asador. To the rancho. Salute, salute, salute. *Buen provecho.*

Although I do not remember her, many stories carry the legend of the aunt who made the most delicate tortillas. After spending hours before the big wood stove in the kitchen, Aunt Emma would sit in a special chair placed to the side of the long dining tables so that she could personally give out her famous tortillas – only given out at request and never, never placed on the tables to mingle with the stacks of Other Tortillas. Each person desiring one of Aunt Emma's tortillas had to go where she sat with them securely and possessively on her lap.

The food was bountiful and there was never a concern if a few more guests should unexpectedly arrive. This was in keeping with the days when tired riders would stop at ranchos for food and drink for there were no inns or hotels; although it was considered rude to travel without your own knife to cut your meat. A guest, suddenly appearing at mealtime, could say, *"Más vale que llegar a tiempo que ser invitado,"* or "It is better to arrive on time than to be invited." Old Spanish proverb.

The eating seemed to go on for hours at the festive barbeques. The food was savored and discussed. Afterwards, the men smoked and the women cleared the tables. The guests wandered off again to drift into the trees or down the road toward town, the real world.

During the early days of the ranch, as often recounted by Grandpa and his brothers, the barbeque was only part of the usual festivities. Often there was a week of dancing and merriment or perhaps a bear and bull fight, a sport which was to die off in the 1850's.

Our family, like most Early California families, has its own bear story handed down to each generation like a priceless heirloom. Grizzly bears were abundant in Early California and it was not uncommon for them to wander into town for a nibble or about the grounds of the ranchos. But as Grandpa told the story, our grizzly bear entered Rancho Los Tularcitos in grand style.

One afternoon, when several women were busy working in the kitchen adobe near the creek, a bear fell through the thatched roof. He was only trying to reach a particularly succulent wild plum at the very top of the tree overhanging the adobe. Screaming women ran out of the house, leaving it to the bear. Horses were always kept ready, with riatas coiled at the saddle bow so several of the men jumped on their steeds and surrounded the perplexed bear who, by now, had come out of the house. The grizzly was swiftly lassoed and tied to a nearby sycamore tree, the best kind of tree for securing bears.

Excited over capturing the bear, the men of Los Tularcitos sent messengers to neighboring ranchos to announce the staging of a bear and bull fight and, of course, a barbeque.

Whenever I heard this story as a child I felt immensely sorry for the bear who only sought the perfect plum at the top of the tree, and unwittingly provided an excuse for another fiesta. The plum bear did lose the fight to the bull as did many other grizzlies, before and after, who roamed the Diablo foothills near the rancho.

Since grizzlies were thought of as frightening intruders, the bear and bull fights were encouraged. Customarily, the hindfoot of the bear was tied to the forefoot of the bull in order to equalize the battle. Grandpa told us of one grizzly presumed dead who was left unattended after a fight. The bear sneaked off during the revelry and was later spotted in the foothills, his wounds stuffed with grass. This bear, having wisely doctored himself, made us feel happier about his ending and we always begged to hear his story after that of the plum bear.

We grew up listening to numerous tales of life on the rancho, told many times over so that we always knew the ending, but it was these traditions along with the ones we actually experienced, like the barbeques, that made us feel proud of the heritage of the rancho.

The bull's head barbeque was saved for very special occasions as it took more time than the usual Sunday barbeque and a large group of people had to gather the day before to attend to the digging of the pit and the lighting and keeping of the fires.

BULL'S HEAD BARBEQUE

Necessary Items:

Smooth stones
Hardwood and kindling
Shovels, at least 3
Long-handled hook
Burlap sacks, 2
Muslin
Baling wire
Heavy gloves
Metal sheet or tarp to cover pit
Wheelbarrow
Heavy board on which to serve bull's head

Ingredients:

1 Bull's Head
Bunches of fresh mint,
 oregano and
 rosemary

Due to its great size the bull's head was always cooked in a pit. The pit, four feet square and four feet deep, was dug in a large open area the day before the barbeque when enough men were present to share in the task. To make tending the fires and getting the cooked head back out of the pit an easier job, the men dug a ledge around the pit, at least two feet down from ground level and two feet wide.

While some were making the pit, others were sent to search for smooth stones from the creek bed near the ranch house. The stones were piled in a deep layer at the bottom of the pit. At the peak of the fire the stones became red hot, retained the heat and were the key to the success of the primitive oven.

On the ranch, for a bull's head, the fire was started with kindling the night before the barbeque – from 15 to 20 hours ahead of serving time. The meat was served at midday the next afternoon. For five hours during the night hard wood was added continually to the fire. Usually, there was one particular man who was the chief, and only he judged when the coals were hot and thick enough to receive the meat. For his lifetime, my grandfather occupied that position of honor and it was one of the joys of his life.

Meanwhile, the feeding of the fire and the collecting of the walnut wood was one of the most important parts of the ritual, usually nursed along by a comradely group of men sipping glasses of red wine and beer. The group sustained itself into the long, cool hours of the morning with endless stories. The women got up early and with them came the beautiful smell of fresh coffee. They served a good breakfast of eggs, bacon and ham, potato rolls - a macho breakfast as the bull's head barbeque was part of the rites of machismo.

Tending of the Bull's Head

The head was thoroughly washed down with buckets of cold water or a garden hose. Of course, all the hair was left decorously on the head with bouquets of mint, oregano and rosemary stuffed into the ears and mouth. The children loved to help with this part.

First, the bull's head was wrapped in wet muslin and then in wet burlap secured well by baling wire bound in several directions. Between 5 and 6:00 a.m. came the high point of the ceremony when they lowered the head onto the hot stones of the pit. They then covered the head with criss-crossed palm leaves in a thick layer. In later days they used a metal sheet. This covering sealed in the heat and kept the dirt from falling on the meat. Next, they quickly shoveled on an even layer of dirt to further seal the heat in the pit. The dirt was compacted by many strokes of the shovel. The waiting and anticipation helped pass the hours for the assembled guests until the head was cooked, about 7 to 8 hours.

Everyone gathered around the pit for the unearthing. A wheelbarrow or cart was waiting nearby. Two men carefully shoveled dirt off the pit. Using shovels and a hook they removed the hot metal sheet and reached the wrapped bundle. The head was lifted out and placed into the wheelbarrow, which the chief quickly took to a grassy place where he unwrapped the head before his mesmerized audience. His deft gloved hands removed the baling wire and burlap to reveal the bull's head. The eyes of the bull were tokens given the chief along with the cheeks which were a succulent delicacy. The children waited for the huge set of teeth so they could run off to frighten any squeamish young ladies on the sidelines. The cook then lifted the head onto a large wooden board garnished with fresh herbs. The meat was pulled off with a fork and served with freshly made sarsa (recipe follows).

PIT BARBEQUE

If you shy away from the bull's head for your pit barbeque, you might try other favorite cuts of beef, such as beef shoulder or beef chuck roasts. You should choose a chunk of meat weighing from twenty-five to twenty-seven pounds to make your rewards worth the effort it takes to cook in a pit. Because it is a method of steam cooking the meat cooks rapidly for its size. The greatest error you can make is to leave the meat too long so that it becomes mushy. If you start the meat at 6:00 a.m., it will be ready for lunch. Whether you cook one twenty-five pound roast, or several, you will need to go to almost the same amount of trouble, needing the same tools.

With the beef roast, as opposed to the bull's head, you can use more seasonings such as given below for one twenty-five pound, boned and tied chuck. Rub the following dry marinade on the meat several hours ahead:

1/3 cup salt

1/4 cup pepper

8 - 10 cloves garlic put through press or minced

3 tablespoons minced dry oregano

    OR   6 tablespoons fresh oregano

1 tablespoon chile powder

1.   Just before placing the meat in the pit, wrap it in cheesecloth that has been soaked in dry red wine. Next, wrap in heavy aluminum foil.

2.   Wrap in soaked burlap and secure with baling wire.

3.   Lower the meat onto the hot coals and stones.

4.   Cover with heavy tarp or metal sheet as described in bulls' head barbeque.

5.   Cover with 1 1/2 feet of tamped dirt. Make sure there is no sign of steam escaping from the pit as this is an indication the meat could be burning. The chief cook usually checks the pit several times for telltale signs of steam. Dirt is shoveled over any steam vents.

6.   Cook for 7 hours.

7.   Uncover as given in directions for bull's head. Cut meat on edged chopping board so as not to lose the juices. Slice across the grain. Serve with fresh, picante tomato sarsa, beans, tortillas and hunks of bread. On the ranch the meat was often served with strips of green chile peppers that had been roasted and skinned.

This is a wonderful way to cook meat for a large crowd as everyone enjoys the primitiveness of the method. It would be reasonable to cook a 25 pound roast in a small pit for a guest list of 20 people. The pit-steamed meat goes with a variety of sauces and is perfect as a basis for Mexican foods such as burritos if you have leftovers.

There were always bowls of sarsa, the old California Spanish colloquialism meaning salsa, on the table to accompany barbequed meats. We spooned it over beans, into burritos, and for a surprising change, it is wonderful to spread over hunks of French bread to accompany a glass of wine. In the northern parts of the continent the English colonists refused to eat the tomato, believing it to possess wicked, magical powers; whereas the Californios readily accepted the love apple. Sarsa was where the tomato found itself most often.

Sarsas and salsas give the cook freedom for creativity. Add what's in season – sweet bermuda onions, white onions, purple Mexican garlic, tomatoes from your garden. All ingredients are appropriate. *"Cada cocinero se le cae un tomate entero,"* or "Sooner or later every cook will drop a whole tomato." In that case, put it in the sarsa or salsa. Green onions are never added to salsa in Mexico, but I always include them; and sometimes three different fresh chiles – anaheims, jalapenos and serranos – find their way into my salsa. If you lack some of the fresh ingredients it's perfectly all right to doctor your sarsa with bottled salsa or pepper flakes.

CHUNKY HOT SALSA

1 pound fresh tomatoes, peeled, seeded, roughly chopped
1 onion chopped
1 bunch green onions, chopped
2 cloves garlic, minced
3 to 8 serrano chiles
    flamed, peeled, seeds removed and minced
2 tablespoons vegetable oil
2 tablespoons vinegar
1 or 2 tablespoons fresh cilantro, chopped
salt to taste

Mix all ingredients together and serve to accompany barbequed steaks, enchiladas, burritos, tacos – or take as a restorative.

RANCHO SARSA

3 - 4 large, ripe tomatoes
(peeled, seeded and chopped - do not put in blender
or food processor)
3 - 4 California chiles (peeled, seeded and chopped)
1/2 onion, minced
1 - 2 jalapeño chiles (canned is fine) minced
1 tablespoon fresh cilantro, snipped
(optional, but excellent)
1 tablespoon cider vinegar
1 teaspoon fresh oregano (optional)
1 clove garlic, minced

Blister the tomatoes over a gas flame or place under the broiler for about twenty minutes. Sear the skin so it slips off easily. If good tomatoes are out of season, substitute canned, Italian plum tomatoes. Do not use anemic, pink tomatoes. Flame and peel chiles or use Ortega green chiles. Combine the chopped tomatoes, chiles, onion, garlic, cilantro, oregano and vinegar. Allow sarsa to mellow in the refrigerator for at least one hour before using - although I have been known to eat it by the spoonful immediately after putting it together. It keeps well for a day, but will start to lose its fresh taste after that. Sarsa that has been heated (without the fresh herbs), to take away the raw flavor, is perfect to spoon over huevos rancheros. If your sarsa seems to be watery due to the quality of the tomatoes, you may bind it together with a few tablespoons of canned tomato puree.

CARNE ASADA

The most favored meat to cook on the parillas was flank or top sirloin which had been cut horizontally to obtain thin steaks, or whole chuck roasts. Fresh garlic was minced with fresh oregano, salt and finely ground pepper. The meat was rubbed generously with the above marinade of herbs and garlic and placed in stoneware crocks in a cool place, but never refrigerated. You may rub your meat with the marinade at least 24 hours in advance and keep it refrigerated; several hours before you are planning on barbequing, leave out the meat in a cool spot in your kitchen. Meat should not be ice cold when placed on a grill.

Most frequently, due to the abundance of wood from the walnut orchard and the vineyard, the fires were started with grapewood and sustained with the hard walnut wood which gives long-lasting coals, not burning away quickly. Mesquite charcoal from Mexico is currently in fashion for barbequing as it gives a wonderful smoky flavor. At any rate, it is best to use wood for your barbeque but if you must use charcoal, do not use starter fluid for it gives a distasteful chemical flavor to the meat. You may purchase handy electrical starter units to help you out. Keep a bottle of water with a sprinkler top or, as Grandpa, a stick with a rag on the end so you can douse any flames. Often times a quiet bed of whitened coals will flame up from the fat dripping off the meat.

When your coals are white, place your meat on the grills, moving it from side to side for the first few minutes so it will not stick. The timing is up to your discretion and the cut of meat you are using.

Carne asada was always served with fresh sarsa and sometimes green chiles that had been flamed and peeled and cut into strips.

Grandmama made a lovely fresh, green sauce which was used only with barbequed steaks. The only other place I've ever tasted it was in an Argentine restaurant in Mexico City where miniature barbeques, like the Japanese hibachis, were brought to our table for us to tend our own steak. This procedure, along with a pitcher of sangria, made us quite happy. The chimichuri sauce was in little stoneware pots and we used up several pots, so delighted were we at our find.

This green sauce, which seemed to have no California origin, reminded me once again of Grandmama and Grandpa's South American heritage – as each of them had one parent who had come from Chile to California to seek the streets lined with gold.

CHIMICHURI SAUCE FOR BARBEQUED STEAKS

1/4 cup finely minced parsley (Italian parsley is best)
1 teaspoon dried oregano
        OR   1 tablespoons fresh oregano
2 cloves garlic, minced
2 tablespoons onion, minced
salt and freshly ground pepper
1/2 cup olive oil
1/4 cup vinegar

I like to place all the fresh herbs and garlic on a chopping board and, using a sharp knife, mince everything together until it is very finely chopped. Lastly, place in a bowl and stir in the oil and vinegar, salt and pepper to taste. Allow it to mellow for a few hours before using.

BUTTERFLIED LAMB IN POMEGRANATE JUICE

The soaked fresh herbs, tossed into the fire at the last minute, and the pomegranate juice give the meat an exotic flavor.

1 6 pound leg of lamb, boned and butterflied
2 - 3 cups pomegranate juice (may be purchased bottled at
        health food stores)
3 tablespoons fresh rosemary, bruised to release oils
        OR use 1 tablespoon dried rosemary

4 garlic cloves, cut into slivers
salt to taste and freshly ground pepper
branches of green rosemary or oregano
(soak in water before placing on the coals)

Cut slits in the meat and stuff in slivers of garlic on both sides. Be sure that you trim off all the fell and fat, exposing the meat. The marinade will penetrate better and there will not be the strong, lamb flavor often caused by fat residue. Place the meat in a shallow dish and rub with rosemary and fresh pepper. Add the pomegranate juice and marinate for at least 6 hours in the refrigerator. Turn the meat occasionally so the marinade will penetrate all surfaces. Bring the meat to room temperature before barbequing or roasting.

For barbeque:

The coals should be covered by white ash with the grill placed 4 - 5 inches above the heat of the fire. Place the meat flat on the hot grill, brushing with the marinade frequently. For rare meat you will need to grill the lamb about 20 minutes per side and 30 minutes per side for medium rare (135 degrees on a meat thermometer). During the last 10 minutes of grilling, place some of the soaked branches of green herbs on the coals. The herbal oils released into the smoke will delicately flavor the meat. This is an old trick of Grandpa's. Sometimes he would toss in old garlic hulls and skins. At this time, you may also salt and pepper the meat and remove from the grill when it is done to your preference, but allow it to rest at least 10 minutes before carving. This grilled lamb is particularly good with Pesto Vegetables on the Grill (see index).

Beans were an everyday food to the Early Californians and must be included in this chapter because they were always eaten with the barbequed meats. *"Frijoles, frijolitos, y frijoles refritos."* Beans, beans, and leftover beans. Beans were a godsend in hungry times. Everyone loved them and the women were religious about the way they should be cooked. Grandmama insisted the tiny pink beans had the best flavor and they should never, never be hurried along by overnight soaking which would only sap away the flavor of the beans. Below are two recipes. The first is Grandmama's Beans, simple with the ingredients and never altered over fifty years. They were started in the morning and spooned into fresh flour tortillas for hungry children's lunches or snacks. When Grandmama proclaimed them "almost done," anyone in the kitchen under ten years old would run for a bowl and she would make for them a bean salad by sprinkling olive oil, vinegar, salt and pepper over a ladleful of warm beans whose broth had not yet been thickened.

27

Grandmama's Beans, although part of the everyday fare, were always served at every barbeque and festive occasion.

1 pound pink beans
2 ham hocks
1 onion, chopped
2 cloves garlic
1 tablespoon powdered red chile
salt to taste
   (to be added the last 1/2 hour of cooking)

Rinse beans well in colander and pick over for stones. Start beans with cold water to cover. Add the ham hocks, onion, garlic and chile powder. Simmer gently for four hours, adding boiling water if necessary to keep the beans from drying out. Our beans were always eaten with a thick broth so you must mash at least a cup of beans, removed from the pot, in a little bowl using a wooden spoon or you may mash them against the side of the pot. Stir the thickened beans back into the pot. If the broth does not seem thick enough, mash more beans. Add salt during the last half hour of cooking.

A friend in San Luis Obispo cooks beans every year for a crowd of eighty people that come for a fiesta on her ranch. These beans are acclaimed as much as Grandmama's version.

FANCY BEANS WITH CHILES

1 pound pink pinquito beans

> *(some of the best beans I have ever tasted; they are grown along the California coast near San Luis Obispo, but plain pink beans will do)*

1 pound ham hocks
2 - 3 tablespoons olive oil
2 medium onions, chopped
2 cloves garlic, minced
1 large can green chiles, diced
1 7 ounce can green chile salsa

> *(do not add salsa if you plan on refrying leftover beans later)*

salt to taste, added after several hours cooking time
freshly ground pepper to taste

In a large skillet saute in hot olive oil the minced garlic, the chopped onions and the ham hocks until the onions are softened. Place the beans, which you have rinsed and picked over for stones, in a large pot. Add the onion, garlic and ham hocks and cover with cold water. If the beans should seem to need more liquid, always add hot water. After two hours of simmering, add the minced chiles and salsa. Simmer for at least a couple of hours more, adding salt to taste during the last half hour of cooking. Taste the beans first, as the ham hocks will add salt also.

Red enchiladas, one of the most typical of the rancho foods, were always found in great abundance at barbeques. There were pans and pans of them to accompany the grilled meats. Enchiladas were such a favorite of *las comidas del pais* (the native foods), eaten any time of day, they were insolently called Spanish cakes by the foreigners from Boston. The tradition of enchiladas in the morning survived in our family and I can remember breakfasts of coffee with lots of sugar and Pet milk and an enchilada bearing on its middle, a sizzled egg with curly edges – to make you grow up strong. As Grandmama and Mama gave you food, you were always reminded of lengthening bones, gleaming hair, and the long legs you would have if you ate all they placed before you. At the same time Mama would take me aside to warn that all the coffee I drank at Grandmama's table was going to stunt my growth.

The red enchiladas below are one of my favorite family foods. Do not underestimate the simplicity of the ingredients. The onions are especially good because you will saute them slowly until they are quite sweet. Because flour tortillas are used, the enchiladas are so light they will often puff up like miniature souffles.

RED ENCHILADAS

3 cups red chile sauce (see below)
10 large flour tortillas, preferably homemade
    (see recipe index. Do not use corn tortillas.
5 medium onions, finely chopped

3 tablespoons olive oil

1 1/2 pounds sharp Cheddar cheese
    or domestic Greek Kasseri, grated

1 large can pitted, black olives

Cook the onions slowly in hot olive oil for 1/2 hour until they are very soft, but not browned. This step is crucial to the recipe. Warm the red chile sauce in a wide, flat pan so you may dip one tortilla at a time into the sauce until it is completely masked. Lay it on a flat dinner plate and place down the center about 1/4 cup cheese, 2 tablespoons onion and two or three black olives. Fold over the sides and gently lift the huge enchilada, seam side down, into a long, greased pan. You can assemble these the day before you want to serve them, but they will absorb much of the sauce. Sprinkle a few tablespoons of sauce over the enchiladas just before heating in a 350 degree oven for about 20 minutes or until the cheese is bubbling.

If you want a more artistic effect, just before you bake the enchiladas create a latticework of cheese strips and black olives over the top. Remember not to add too much additional sauce to the baking pan or you are likely to end up with a casserole of broken enchiladas.

RED CHILE SAUCE

3 tablespoons oil

3 tablespoons flour

1 clove garlic, mashed with 1 teaspoon salt

1 teaspoon dried oregano

3 cups chile puree (see recipe index for instructions
pureeing dried, red chiles)
OR 1 large can of Las Palmas red chile sauce

2 tablespoons vinegar

Heat oil in a heavy skillet and add flour, stirring constantly until the roux is golden (it will lose its raw taste). Add the rest of the ingredients and simmer for 20 - 30 minutes to meld the flavors. If you use the canned red chile sauce, it will need the same amount of simmering, but will provide you with a delicious result. If you puree your own chiles your resulting sauce will be thicker and have a stronger, more robust flavor than if you use the canned sauce as a base.

On the ranch certain dishes were traditional and one did not sway from the pathway. The elders happily consumed pans of enchiladas always made in the same way, filled with sauteed onions, cheese and olives. In our family a new daughter-in-law who filled her enchiladas with hamburger was spoken of in hushed tones. And now I fill mine with eggplant, venturing off into that Latin world of endless variations on enchiladas. The chunks of eggplant are often mistaken for meat and someone always asks for the recipe.

EGGPLANT ENCHILADAS

12 corn tortillas
oil

For sauce:

6 - 8 chiles, anchos or pasillas
1 clove of garlic mashed with 1 teaspoon salt
2 tablespoons olive oil + 2 tablespoons flour
1 teaspoon dried oregano

Filling:

1 eggplant, peeled and diced
2 onions, chopped
3 teaspoons oregano
2 1/2 cups sharp Cheddar, grated
freshly ground black pepper
salt to taste

Toast the dried chiles a few at a time in a heavy iron skillet. Do not burn or they will develop a bitter taste. When cool, break up chiles to remove stems and seeds. Rinse under cool water. Place in a large bowl and cover with boiling water. Let the chiles steep for at least one hour. Place the soaked chiles in a blender jar along with one cup of the soaking liquid. Puree. If the resulting puree is too thick, add more soaking liquid. Toast the flour in the olive oil until golden, then add the chile puree, the garlic, oregano and salt. Simmer for 10 minutes.

For the filling, saute the onions in oil until they are very soft but not browned (about 20 minutes). Meanwhile, place eggplant cubes in vegetable steamer and steam for 8 minutes. Blot off excess moisture and place in the same saute pan as the onions, cooking together for another 10 minutes or until eggplant is fork-tender. Add the oregano, salt and pepper.

To prepare the tortillas, heat oil in a cast-iron skillet. Fry the tortillas for just a few seconds until softened. Or you may soften the tortillas by placing them in a hot skillet, nonstick or cast-iron, and heat, turning once. Do not heat too long or they will dry out. Heat tortilla only until it softens.

Dip each softened tortilla in the warm sauce and place on a flat dinner plate. Down the center, place a couple of tablespoons of cheese and a couple of tablespoons of the eggplant-onion mixture. Roll up and place in a long, greased baking dish. Bake at 350 degrees or until cheese is bubbly. To finally break all of Grandmama's rules, I like to garnish these with sour cream or yogurt that has been blended with some minced green onion.

When my husband and I were honeymooning in a lovely, colonial house in San Miguel de Allende, Mexico, the cook prepared us Swiss Enchiladas, her specialty, but I was such a moonstruck bride I did not request the recipe or even peek into the kitchen - for once in my life. To come closer to the delicate, fine flavor of Nasha's enchiladas, I began making crepes, using part masa harina in place of the corn tortillas. The enchiladas are covered with homemade *crème fraîche* the closest substitute for the thick Mexican double cream. The colonial house is sold and Nasha gone with her recipe, but my husband says these enchiladas are the right ones.

SWISS CREAM ENCHILADAS

12 to 14 corn masa crepes:

> *1/2 cup masa harina, Quaker brand*
> *2 tablespooons white flour*
> *3 eggs*
> *1 cup milk (may need to add 1/4 cup more milk*
> > *if batter is too thick)*
> *3 tablespoons butter, melted*
> *1/2 teaspoon salt*

Place ingredients in blender jar in the order listed. Blend until well mixed. Let the batter rest in the refrigerator for one hour and then put through a wire sieve as the masa harina tends to settle to the bottom. Add more milk if the batter has thickened. Heat crepe pan or small six-inch skillet, brush with oil and pour in a scant 1/4 cup crepe batter. Cook until slightly golden, shaking pan, loosen edges of crepe with knife, and turn. As you cook each crepe, stack between pieces of waxed paper. Give the crepe batter a stir from time to time.

Filling for Swiss Cream Enchiladas:

3 whole chicken breasts

2 cans chicken broth (or about 3 cups homemade)

1 carrot, sliced

1 onion, cut in quarters

1 sprig cilantro

1 can of green chiles, seeded and cut into strips

2 1/2 cups mild white cheese like Monterey Jack

   (I like to use part Italian Fontina and part Jack)

2 cups homemade crème fraîche (directions follow)

   (sour cream is NOT adequate in this recipe)

pimiento strips for optional garnish

sprigs of cilantro for optional garnish

Twenty-four hours before you will need the creme fraiche, add 2 tablespoons buttermilk to one pint of heavy cream. Stir well. Leave in a warm spot to thicken in a glass bowl for eight to twelve hours, depending on temperature of the room. It should appear as thick as sour cream, but remember it will thicken more after it is refrigerated.

Place the chicken breasts in a three quart pot and cover them with the broth, sliced carrot, onion and cilantro, adding water if necessary, to keep them completely submerged. Bring to a simmer and poach gently for 18 minutes. Remove from heat and allow chicken to cool in the broth for 1/2 hour. Remove the skin and bones. Cut into long pieces to fit in enchiladas. Grate the cheese and cut the green chiles into strips and drain.

Have ready two greased, long baking dishes so you may place seven enchiladas in each one. Lay crepe out flat and fill with several pieces of chicken, a couple of strips of chile and 2 tablespoons of cheese. Roll up and place in dish. When all the enchiladas are in baking dishes, pour the thickened cream over the top. Reserve 1/4 cup of the *crème fraîche* . Heat enchiladas for 20 minutes in 350 degree oven. Cream is quickly absorbed into the crepes so do not overheat as the enchiladas will dry out. Before serving, drizzle the reserved creme fraîche over the top and garnish with pimiento and cilantro.

MIGAS

Migas were usually made with day-old sourdough bread. The recipe was always varied depending on what was at hand. Sometimes there was no fresh bacon available so just garden herbs were used.

1 pound loaf sourdough or French bread, day-old

3 cloves garlic, minced

1 medium onion, finely chopped

1/2 cup crumbled fried bacon or chorizo sausage

2 teaspoons parsley, minced

1 teaspoon dried oregano

1 teaspoon dry basil

1/2 teaspoon pepper, freshly ground

1 teaspoon salt

---

1 cup water

1 tablespoon vinegar

For frying migas:

1 cup olive oil

5 cloves garlic, mashed

heavy cast-iron frying pan

Using a bread knife or serrated knife, shave very thin pieces of bread off loaf. Do not cut off complete slices. Place the bread pieces in large bowl with onion, garlic, bacon, herbs, and seasonings. Sprinkle with vinegar - water. Cover and set aside to marinate for several hours. The mashed garlic should be placed in a cup of olive oil several hours in advance of cooking the migas. When you are ready to prepare the migas, remove the garlic cloves. Heat 1/4 cup of the garlic oil in a cast-iron or heavy skillet. Place enough bread in skillet to cover the bottom in a thin layer. Reserve the rest of the bread mixture as it will take four separate fryings to prepare the whole batch of migas. Push and flatten the migas until like a pancake. You might have to add a little garlic oil around the edges of the skillet. When the migas pancake is golden brown, slide onto a flat plate, add a couple of tablespoons of garlic oil to the skillet and flip the migas back so the other side may be browned. Once your cast-iron skillet is hot, you will only need to add one tablespoon of oil at a time. Serve the migas while warm. Everyone can break off pieces from the communal pancake. Serves 8 - 10. These crisp, garlicky croutons are wonderful with soup, chile, or barbequed meats.

Versions of this recipe have been passed around from family to family because it's another good way to freshen up a stale loaf or make a fresh loaf taste good. I could easily make a meal off pan relleno and a glass of wine.

PAN RELLENO

1 loaf sourdough or French bread, cut in half lengthwise
1 cup sharp, finely grated cheese - Cheddar or
    Monterey Jack
1/3 cup onion, chopped
1 clove garlic, minced
2 tablespoons olive oil
4 tablespoons butter

1 tablespoon vinegar
1/4 cup chopped olives
aluminum foil

Blend all ingredients together. If you use a food processor do not puree the olives and onions. Spread on each half of loaf. Wrap tightly in foil. Bake in 350 degree oven for 15 - 20 minutes until cheese is melted and loaf is good and hot.

PESTO VEGETABLES ON THE GRILL

Often when Grandpa was barbequing butterflied leg of lamb in the summer months, he would also grill fresh vegetables, but only when the most exquisite vegetables could be gathered from the garden - tomatoes, Spanish onions, zucchini, Anaheim chile peppers, bell peppers and corn. The cleaned vegetables would be brushed with olive oil and placed on the parilla - either whole or in halves. One summer evening, while contemplating a leftover half cup of pesto sauce, I was inspired to brush it on the vegetables about to be grilled and a family favorite was born. Hereafter, all grilling vegetables are swathed in pesto sauce.

Pesto Sauce:

2 cups fresh basil leaves
3/4 cup olive oil
3 tablespoons soft butter

2 tablespoons pine nuts (optional)

3/4 cup Parmesan cheese

3 cloves garlic

1 teaspoon salt

freshly ground pepper

Grind all of the above ingredients in a blender or food processor. The sauce will keep in the refrigerator for about three days. Do not freeze. You can feeze the herbs and oil (see recipe index for Basil Oil) and when you are ready to make pesto sauce, place the basil oil in the blender with the rest of the above ingredients.

Preparing vegetables for the grill:

1 huge red onion, halved

2 Anaheim or California green chiles, whole

3 green peppers, halved

4 small zucchini, halved

4 small tomatoes, whole

4 ears corn, silk removed,
   but green husks intact (optional)

Place the vegetables on the grill, over whitened coals, in the order given (except the fresh corn). The onion, peppers, bell peppers and corn require the most time – at least 20 minutes. While grilling, brush with pesto sauce. Keep turning the vegetables so they cook evenly. The oil will cause the surface to char a little, but that is what we like.

MY GARDEN'S GAZPACHO

Somewhere there is an esoteric version of Spanish gaz-pacho but I adhere to the one dictated by my garden with some inspiration from M. F. K. Fisher's gazpacho. The secret is to start with an herbal base, almost like a pesto sauce. Then you add chilled tomato juice and finally a myriad of chopped vegetables, creating a floating island. Gazpacho is a good accompaniment to barbequed meat or for the first course of the evening meal.

Herbal Base:

2 garlic cloves mashed with 1/2 teaspoon salt

1 tablespoon chives, snipped

5 leaves fresh basil, snipped

> *OR: use 2 teaspoons Basil Oil (see recipe index)*

2 tablespoons parsley, chopped

2 scallions, chopped

juice from 1 lemon

1/4 cup olive oil

freshly ground pepper to taste

Tabasco sauce to taste

reserve 4 - 5 cups chilled tomato juice

Place all of the above ingredients except tomato juice into a blender and roughly puree to form the herbal base. Then add 4 - 5 cups of chilled tomato juice.

Gazpacho Vegetables:

3 beautiful, ripe tomatoes (peeled, seeded, chopped)

2 cucumbers, peeled and chopped

1 red Spanish onion, chopped finely

1 avocado, diced (optional)

1 zucchini, diced

Stir the chopped vegetables into the liquid base. Place the gazpacho in a glass, or better yet, a crystal bowl and sprinkle with more minced herbs such as parsley or chives. If you have leftover tomato juice, you may pour it into an ice cube tray and freeze. Float the tomato cubes in the gazpacho when serving. Migas are a lovely accompaniment to this chilled soup-salad, which you could also pack to a picnic in glass jars.

A discussion of flour tortillas must be included along with all the other trimmings of the barbeque. There could be no barbeque without tortillas.

In Early California flour was so scarce tortillas were only eaten on special occasions. As more wheat was cultivated, ranchos like our own, milled their grain and flour became available for everyday use. During a barbeque or fandango, five or six women would be kept busy turning out flour tortillas in a constant flow.

The Californio used tortillas in preference to bread. A triangle of tortilla, held with thumb and second finger, became a shovel. The children in our family were taught to make little tents to scoop up food before being introduced to more civilized utensils.

The use of the tortilla became an art in itself. You can roll one into a cigar shape so as to capture juices left on a plate of carne con chile (not chile con carne). When using a tortilla as a container for juicy morsels or beans, you must fold over the bottom end and sides, cock your head sideways and bite with your teeth, not your lips. If you squeeze with your lips, you will be caught with juices running down your shirtfront.

Each girl who married into the family had to learn the art of tortilla making from one of the masters such as Grandmama or Aunt Nicolassa or, before her, Aunt Emma. Since the beginner was taught to stretch the tortilla by hand, similar to the way a pizza maker stretches his dough, the first attempts had the look of freeform art. On one legendary rancho these were called violins.

You must try making tortillas on a day when you feel unhurried and you can work to get the feel of the dough, rolling it a little, stretching it, and most important, being unafraid of it. So it is just as well you don't have an aunt who is famous for her light-as-a-handkerchief tortillas breathing down your neck.

FLOUR TORTILLAS

4 cups all-purpose flour, unbleached
1 1/2 teaspoon salt
2 rounded tablespoons shortening (Crisco)
1 1/4 to 1 1/2 cups warm water

Dissolve the salt in the 1 1/4 cups of warm water. Reserve the rest of the water to be added only if necessary. Blend shortening into the flour until mealy. Add warm water slowly until you have a soft dough. You may need to add a little more water. Knead the dough for about a minute in the bowl. Let it rest for 20 minutes under plastic wrap and then break it off and form 16 flat balls. Keep the balls under a piece of plastic wrap so they do not dry out and let rest 10 minutes.

The art of rolling out each ball into a thin circle will be accomplished with a little practice. Have your comal or griddle getting hot while you begin rolling the first tortilla.

Place one ball of dough on a pastry board. Keeping an even pressure on your floured rolling pin, roll out a thick circle. The dough should grip the board. Now using short, quick strokes with the rolling pin, roll from the center to the edge of your tortilla and keep turning it so the circle stays even. Roll from the center, give a quarter turn. As you roll, you must stretch out the circle. The best rolling pin is a 5 inch sawed-off piece of broomstick. Tortillas are not as delicate as pastry so do not apply the same principles. Do not worry if a few wrinkles develop as you roll. If you can't smooth them out keep them. As Grandmama always said, wrinkles show character.

Your tortilla should be thin, about 10 inches wide. Hold it up and pull the fingers of one hand across the width of the tortilla to pull and stretch it a little. Next, pull your fingers across in the other direction to keep your circle even. Grandmama always used the thumbs and forefingers of both hands to further stretch the tortilla. You can do this too, but you can make perfectly delicious tortillas using just a rolling pin to make them thin.

Place your tortilla on the hot griddle. Leave only 15 - 20 seconds before turning. The trick is to not put your fingers next to the griddle, but to push your forefinger into the far side of the tortilla to get a grip and turn.

Keep turning the tortilla every 10 to 15 seconds for about a minute. Do not cook it too long or it will become dry. By shifting the tortilla, you will be adjusting for hot spots on your griddle. Place the tortilla in a tea towel or foil immediately if you can resist eating this first one smeared with butter. Roll out and cook the next tortilla.

The above directions may seem exceedingly long but tortilla making is an art, at once simple and yet difficult for someone who has never seen it done. And the directions must take the place of the masterful aunt.

Flour tortillas will keep well for several days if wrapped in foil. They are delicious for breakfast, toasted under a broiler with sharp Cheddar on top, like an open-faced quesadilla.

To freshen up store-bought or stale tortillas, place on a hot griddle and keep turning until they become soft and fragile again.

A picture of the family taken from the second floor of the main adobe. Maria Higuera is to the far right.

CHAPTER III

THE QUIET DAYS OF THE WEEK

 can remember sitting at the kitchen table of the ranchhouse with Grandpa, the kerosene lights giving off their faint light, because in the mid-1940's he and my uncles still refused the intrusion of electricity and he would say, "Can you hear the voices singing down The Lane?" "Yes, yes," I would say with reverence for his spirits, "I can hear them." And I did.

In the last century a carriage bearing visitors was ambushed by Indians while it came down The Lane, that ancient grove of olive trees, and the people who had been whiling away their time with Spanish songs, were slaughtered. Their voices, singing as they had been that night, could still be heard coming from The Lane if it was quite dark and one listened very carefully.

The ranch life, in spite of the ghosts, was thought to be healthful for children so the brothers living in town with their families would send out one or two from the flock to keep company with the bachelor uncles and Aunt Nicolassa who let them run free as the squirrels.

If they picked the green apples or peaches and got sick from gorging on them, they simply learned from experience not to do it again. Once when one of the cousins had taken a horse riding into the countryside, he thought it might be an adventure to ride into the tules. The horse hopelessly sunk up to his knees in mud and even with prodding and pushing he could not be moved from the spot. Leaving the animal in his quagmire, the cousin ran back to the ranch for his Uncle John. Two more horses were silently hooked up to the wagon and taken off to pull the horse out of the swamp. Never was a word of chastisement spoken to the boy who felt humiliated.

While their mothers in town hoped for some of the old Spanish ways to rub off, the children sent to the quiet country-side obliged by seeming to stay out of trouble most of the time and being frightened at night by spirits and demonios. Jack, my mother's youngest brother and the youngest of all the cousins, was the most adventurous. He stalked the darkened rooms of the adobe ranchhouse, peering into rooms kept locked for years because of a tragic death. The barn, which was inhabited seasonally by migrant workers who came to help with the fruit, was his domain and he refused to be daunted by creaking noises and footsteps on the stairs at night.

To his delight he found that hornets lived in the tree adjacent to the old adobe wall filled with honey bees and by poking long sticks into the hornets' nest and then into the crumbling wall, the disturbed critters would furiously bombard each other while Jack stood back delighting in the battle.

Days slipped by quietly, with no rush. Since the chickens roamed freely and no one was ever sure where the eggs were, Mama and Jack would scurry around on a daily Easter egg hunt. They knew the chickens loved the cool banks of Calera Creek so they would look there first, sometimes finding a dozen eggs at a time secreted in the tall grass.

Before everyone arrived for the Sunday barbeque, the days proceeded with a quiet pattern of duties – and there was the ritual of sitting on the open verandah in the evening, the uncles smoking after dinner and chatting. Because they loved their songs, they caught red-breasted linnets for pets and kept them in an aviary on the verandah. The linnets were freed in the winter so they could join the flocks of birds heading south.

During the weekdays, when there were no barbeques, they ate simply. For the midday meal, there might be carne con chile, a thick vegetable soup, or a pozole. If someone was ill, a bowl of steaming chicken soup with tiny vermicelli was mandatory medicine.

Some of these comforting, everyday foods are my favorites and the ones I hunger for when I feel a wintery chill or a bad cold coming on – and wish for a glimpse of my olive-skinned grandmother, carrying a tray to me in bed or curled up on the horsehair chesterfield in great need of one of her restoratives.

CHICKEN SOUP WITH VERMICELLI FOR SICK CHILDREN

There are no exact ingredients for this soup as it is dependent upon what you have in the kitchen as you cannot leave a sick child in bed and go off to town and shop.

3 - 4 pounds chicken parts (wings, giblets, neck and backs)
1 clove garlic
1 onion, chopped
2 carrots, scraped if bitter, and sliced
1 inch piece of fresh ginger root (optional)
1 stalk celery, sliced
handful of parsley
1/2 cup vermicelli noodles

Cover chicken parts with cold water in large pot. Using a trick I learned from a Chinese friend, cut the chicken parts into small pieces with an old but well-sharpened knife. These smaller pieces will give up more of their richness to the broth. Skim off foam for the first 20 minutes and then add the rest of the ingredients except vermicelli. Simmer for 3 hours on low heat. Your broth will still be good for pampering body and soul if you lack everything but chicken parts and a few herbs. If you want to be luxurious, simmer a whole, cut-up chicken for 3 hours, removing the breast after 45 minutes. Use the breast for salads, sandwiches, enchiladas, or shred it and put it back into the soup after the broth is strained. Strain the broth through a mesh strainer lined with cheesecloth wrung out in cold water. Often, my own small boys, feeling like their soup will never be done, cannot wait until the broth is defatted the easy way, by chilling in the refrigerator. Do not remove all of the fat as it adds richness and flavor. Place the broth back in the pot to reheat and add two handfuls of the smallest vermicelli you can find. Simmer for 15 minutes, sprinkle with finely minced parsley or green onions and serve to the waiting child, whatever age.

The following soup is one of our favorites, good for a light dinner followed by fresh fruit, and especially endearing to children who love to scoop up the tiny meatballs from the broth. You can make it the long way given below or, by using canned broth and powdered chile, you can make it the fast way. The addition of fresh mint to the ground meat is important.

SOPA DE ALBONDIGAS

Broth

> *3 dried red chiles, California*
>
> *1 onion*
>
> *1 clove garlic plus 1/2 teaspoon comino seeds*
>
> *2 medium tomatoes*
>
>> *OR 2 - 3 canned plum tomatoes*
>
> *6 cups beef or chicken broth (see recipe above for broth)*
>
>> *OR 3 cups stock and 3 cups water*
>
>> *OR 3 cups vegetable stock and 3 cups water*

2 tablespoons olive oil

2 stalks celery, minced

4 carrots, minced

1 potato, minced

1 turnip, minced

Soak the dried chiles, seeded and deveined, in hot water for 45 minutes. Puree in blender with a little soaking liquid and then add the cut up onion, garlic and comino seeds. Puree to heavy sauce consistency. Mince the tomatoes finely. Using a heavy pot, saute the chile mixture in hot olive oil for 2 - 3 minutes. Add the tomatoes and cook away the liquid for 5 minutes on medium heat. Drain off any excess oil that bubbles to the edge. Add the minced vegetables and stock. Simmer for 30 minutes while you prepare the meatballs.

MEATBALLS (ALBONDIGAS)

1 pound ground round

(use lean meat so the soup will not be fatty)

1/4 onion, minced

1 clove garlic, minced

1/4 cup parsley, minced

1/4 cup fresh mint, minced

1/2 cup brown rice, cooked

1 teaspoon oregano

1/2 teaspoon salt

freshly ground pepper

freshly ground nutmeg, only a little

Blend above ingredients with your hands and form into tiny meatballs. After the broth has simmered for 30 minutes, gently add the meatballs and simmer 30 more minutes with lid on. With thick bread for dunking, your meal is complete.

Below is Grandmama's way of making Lentil Soup, my brother's favorite if he felt low as he would have nothing to do with the idea that clear, crystalline broths were needed for healing when what he craved was something thick and hearty.

THICK LENTIL SOUP

2 tablespoons olive oil

6 slices bacon, chopped

1 onion, minced

1 clove garlic, minced

2 green or red bell peppers, minced

4 carrots, scraped and chopped

3 stalks celery, minced

> *OR 1 cup celery root, minced*

16 ounces lentils

3 quarts stock or water

2 cups tomato juice OR tomato puree

salt and pepper to taste

2 ounces diced pimiento (in jar)

Saute the onion, garlic and celery in hot olive oil until softened. Add the rest of the chopped vegetables, the lentils, the broth and tomato juice. Fry bacon in separate pan to render some of the fat and add to the soup. Simmer until tender and the soup is beginning to thicken - about 1 1/2 - 2 hours. Toward the end, add salt and pepper and the diced pimientos. If the soup is too thick, add more tomato juice or water.

This is a colorful and hearty soup that everyone says is quite filling and then they ask for second helpings.

Soups, considered to be everyday fare, were never served for special occasions. One day Mama, who had begun to sway from the path of traditional Spanish-California foods, invented this soup because she had leftover pumpkin puree. I have found it to be a beautiful first course for elegant dinners.

PUMPKIN SOUP FROM MAMA

2 cups steamed pumpkin or acorn squash
    (canned pumpkin can be substituted)
1 1/2 cups strong chicken broth
1 onion, chopped
2 tablespoons butter

1/4 cup finely ground, toasted almonds

pinch of cayenne pepper

salt to taste, freshly ground white pepper

1 cup cream

handful of fresh chives, snipped

3 - 4 strips of bacon, crisply fried (optional)

Cut a small pumpkin into pieces, removing rind and seeds. Place in steamer basket or pot with a couple inches of boiling water. Steam until tender. Remove skin. Meanwhile, saute chopped onion in butter for 20 minutes until it is very soft but not browned. Place the cooked pumpkin and onion in blender or food processor with some of the broth and puree to a smooth consistency. Place the puree back into the pot with the remaining broth – adding the broth a little at a time so your soup does not become too thinned out. Add the ground almonds and seasonings. Simmer for 20 - 30 minutes. The last few minutes, add the cream, being careful the soup does not come to a boil as the cream will separate. Serve the soup garnished with chives and crumbled bacon. If you do not have chives, use minced parsley.

In the bygone days of the ranch when there easily might be ten or fifteen hungry people sitting down to the table for a midday meal, there were some favorite standby dishes meant to be filling. Adding to the mouths to feed was the timely visitor, two or three hours away from the comforts of his own table, and it was only natural he be asked to stay; hence, large pots of

56

stews, by the name *cocidos, pucheros, or olla podridas,* were eaten frequently. The ingredients depended upon what parts of beef were left in the larder, or if someone had shot a few doves or pigeons, or done away with one of the family chickens. Our cocido is different from the traditional one because the brisket is browned, making a richer broth and with the addition of the dried chiles, the broth will develop a deep mahogany color.

SPANISH COCIDO

1 beef brisket, all fat removed

2 - 3 tablespoons olive oil

1 chicken, halved

2 bay leaves

10 peppercorns, crushed

3 cloves garlic, minced

1 onion, chopped

2 dried pasilla chiles,
 broken in half, seeds removed

6 - 8 carrots, scraped

4 potatoes, peeled

1 medium cabbage, quartered

4 leeks, trimmed of dark green part and well rinsed

Assortment of sausages: small pork sausages, kielbasa,
 garlic sausage, or Spanish chorizo
 (use one type or all, depending on what is available)

handful of minced parsley

2 cans garbanzo beans, drained
 OR you may simmer 1 cup dried garbanzos for 2 - 3
  hours in a quart of water, adding more hot water
  if necessary

Brown brisket well in oil on both sides. Remove from pot and add chicken, browning lightly. Remove excess oil. Return brisket to pot, adding the crushed peppercorns, onion, garlic, and dried chiles. Cover with cold water and bring to a boil. Cover and simmer for 1 hour. Remove chicken and reserve. Continue to simmer the beef for at least 1 more hour. Next, add to the pot the carrots, the cooked garbanzos, and the potatoes. Cook until the vegetables are almost tender; stir in the cabbage and leeks. Simmer for 15 - 20 minutes longer. Meanwhile, prepare the sausages by sauteing in a little butter and minced garlic. Keep warm. Place chicken back in pot to reheat.

On a very large platter, arrange the beef brisket in slices with the chicken pieces. Place the sausages in a circle around the chicken and sliced brisket. Ladle some of the hot broth (1/2 cup) over the meats and sprinkle with minced parsley. Artistically surround the meats with your assortment of vegetables –the carrots, potatoes, cabbage, leeks and the garbanzo beans. It should be beautiful. Everyone should be given a big bowl and in our family we pass more of the broth to moisten the brisket and vegetables, but we save the rest of the broth so it can be properly degreased and become the next day's soup. Cocido is a visually stunning dish that should be prepared when you have at least 6 people to keep well-fed.

With beef a major part of the Californians' diet and their beloved chiles an everyday necessity, it was only natural they devise a hearty stew that combined both. Carne con chile (not chile con carne) was one of the most popular dishes on the ranch. In the early days, a big pot of stew would often be found simmering on a stove made only of dirt and adobe bricks with just a sheet of iron for the top. Later, a real kitchen became part of the main ranchhouse and my uncles remember the huge black stove that was as long as a locomotive.

If you wish to make a quicker chile (which we will call gringo chile here), you may substitute coarsely ground beef instead of beef chunks. It will be up to your discretion as to whether you add beans. Within my immediate family, beans in chile were and are an outcast dish, but that does not mean the combination could not be quite savory. Our chile is especially spicy so you can reduce chile amounts and spices for palates with less zest.

CARNE CON CHILE

3 1/2 to 4 pounds chuck roast,
 seven-bone roast or clod roast
 (anything but stew meat), cut into 2 inch chunks
1/4 cup oil
1 medium onion
3 cloves garlic
 cut into pieces and mashed with 1 teaspoon salt
2 teaspoons comino seeds or more,

toasted in cast iron pan, mashed in mortar

(if you do not have a mortar, place seeds between waxed paper and smash with an iron pan or a mallet)

2 teaspoons oregano, toasted in iron pan

2 - 3 teaspoons salt

1 1/2 - 3 cups homemade chile puree (see recipe index)

   OR 1 large can of Las Palmas Red Chile Sauce

2 1/2 cups beef stock

   OR 2 cans beef broth

2 - 4 teaspoons cayenne pepper (optional)

   OR crush a couple of chile pequines and throw in if you like your chile on the HOT side)

2 heaping tablespoons masa harina

1/4 cup water

2 tablespoons chopped fresh cilantro (optional)

black pitted olives for garnish

Dry meat cubes well, using paper towels. In a heavy skillet, preferably cast iron, heat oil until almost smoking and brown cubes of beef in small batches. Use only 1 tablespoon of oil at a time, adding a little more when necessary. Remove cubes of meat as they brown and set aside. In the remaining oil, saute the minced onion and garlic briefly. Drain off excess oil and add beef stock. Return meat cubes to the pan and bring to a simmer, cover tightly and cook slowly for 1 1/2 hours. Drain off all but 1 cup broth. (Use your reserved broth and a little of the leftover chile puree to make sopa de albóndigas the next day.) To this remaining broth and meat, add 1 1/2 cups of chile puree or the canned chile, which is much thinner than homemade puree. Add the herbs and simmer for 1 more hour. Adjust the stew to your taste by adding either more broth or more chile puree. Taste for seasoning and add more herbs or salt to your liking. Blend masa harina with the water to make a paste. Stir into the stew to thicken. Just before serving, stir in the cilantro and black olives. We always need lots of flour tortillas to eat carne con chile - a dunker's delight.

Grandmama would take me as a small child to a tiny, narrow cafe across from St. James Park in San Jose. She would order in Spanish and we would be served carne con chile in big, white bowls. My tongue would burn and my cheeks become red, but at the age of five I became addicted. Carne con chile, like most soul-satisfying stews, necessitates the immediate presence of chunks of crusty bread or tortillas, and something icy cold to drink - beer, Sangria, or even just water. (Serves 6 - 8.)

THE FAMILY STEW

In the aftermath of a bear and bullfight there would be a bull's head barbeque if the bull lost (see Chapter II). Following the festivities, they would make a robust stew for the family to enjoy - after all the guests had gone home. This stew makes one of the richest broths I have ever tasted.

2 1/2 pounds jointed oxtails
    or bull's tail, cut into small sections
1/2 cup flour
    (blended with 1 teaspoon salt, 1/2 teaspoon freshly

> *ground pepper, and one teaspoon paprika, 2 teaspoons*
> *oregano, and 1 teaspoon thyme)*

several tablespoons olive oil

2 medium onions

3 carrots, scraped and sliced

2 cloves garlic, minced

1 bay leaf

1/4 cup brandy

1 cup red wine

2 cups beef or chicken broth

1 long peel of an orange, white pith removed

If the fat around the meat seems excessive, trim it off. Dust the meat in the seasoned flour, patting off excess. Brown a few pieces at a time in hot olive oil. Remove meat as it is browned and add the next batch. Do not crowd it in the pan. In the remaining oil, saute the onion and garlic until softened. Drain off any excess oil and place all the meat back in the pan. Heat the brandy until warm, ignite, and pour the flaming brandy over the meat. This step will not only flavor the meat but burn off excess fat. Now add all the rest of the ingredients except carrots. Simmer on top of the stove for 30 minutes, skimming off any foam which has accumulated. Place in a 325 degree oven for about 3 hours, covered, checking the pot periodically to make sure all the liquid is not evaporating. You can always add a little more wine or broth. This stew is best made the day before it is to be served so the flavors may meld. After refrigeration, skim off any fat on the surface. If the stew has been refrigerated, add the carrots and put it to simmer 30 minutes before serving time. Serve it with plain rice or noodles and bread to dunk in the sauce.

CALIFORNIA POT ROAST WITH BEER

While living in Mexico we often had to concoct dishes using the tough, gamey beef so prevalent there. The favored technique was to brown the roast on both sides, then douse it with a whole can of beer. Covered tightly and baked for a couple of hours, the meat ends up tender and succulent and everyone swears it's the best pot roast they ever tasted. The leftovers are great for making a picadillo to stuff into chiles or for making burritos the next day.

4 pounds beef roast (chuck, seven-bone, rump or brisket)
2 - 4 tablespoons oil
2 onions, chopped
2 whole cloves garlic
1 can of beer
salt and freshly ground pepper to taste

Trim off all fat and dry the meat well with paper towels. Brown well in a heavy cooking pot. The meat should be a deep mahogany brown on all sides. Remove meat from the pot, add more oil if necessary, and brown the chopped onion for about 10 minutes. Drain off any excess oil, return meat to the pot with the onions and garlic and pour in the beer. Place on the lid or cover tightly with a double thickness of aluminum foil. Bake at 350 degrees for 2 1/2 hours. If the broth is not greasy, you may reduce it for a few minutes after you have removed the roast. Serve the broth with the meat or thicken it with potato flour or a regular flour paste for gravy.

On California ranches, beans were eaten several times during the day, but were especially necessary when eating something like carne con chile or shredded pot roast rolled into a tortilla, burrito style; frijoles refritos, or refried beans, absorbed juices and bound morsels together so there was less juice to run down the sleeve.

Frijoles refritos change the character of beans into a toasty, rosy concoction which is the Californios' version of hashed brown potatoes. Unlike the creamy, smooth Mexican refried beans, Grandmama's were quite toasty with a strong hint of sharp cheese and in great demand if there were leftover cold beans from yesterday – and there were always leftover beans in the icebox.

FRIJOLES REFRITOS, REFRIED BEANS CALIFORNIA STYLE

3 cups well-cooked, cold pink beans with thick broth
lard or peanut oil (do not use bacon fat as it is too strong)
dry, grated cheese such as Romano
*   or aged Monterey Jack from California*

Heat two tablespoons of oil in a ten or twelve inch cast iron frying pan until almost smoking. Add beans 1/2 cup at a time, mashing them with a large, wooden spoon. Add more cold beans and a little liquid to the pan, continuing to mash. Fry over medium heat until the frijoles are toasty and beginning to dry at the edges of the pan. Toward the end of frying, sprinkle with the sharp cheese. For a special breakfast, serve frijoles refritos, chorizo sausage and huevos rancheros.

Another staple eaten as frequently as frijoles on the ranch, was chorizo sausage laced with potent combinations of spices and ground chiles so as to disguise the strange combinations of meats necessary in earlier days; although, once the Californios had beef readily available they rarely ate wild game, especially bear meat.

We dearly love chorizo fried and mixed into scrambled eggs for breakfast or snacks. When I was a child, Mama would fix me chorizo and egg sandwiches to appease my constant hunger and many of my peanut-butter-loving playmates became converts to my spicy sandwiches. Chorizo is also wonderful when fried with cubes of potatoes which have been partially boiled first; or, mix chorizo sausage into meatloaf. You must be careful when buying ready-made chorizo in a market as it often contains a huge percentage of fat as well as unmentionable items which is a good reason for making your own sausage.

RANCHO SAUSAGE, CHORIZO

2 pounds lean pork, cut into pieces

10 ounces pork fat, well-chilled and cut into pieces
   (you may lessen the amount of fat by a few ounces –
   the sausage will be drier)

2 cloves garlic, minced

3 teaspoons oregano

1/2 teaspoon black pepper, freshly ground

2 teaspoons comino seeds

3 teaspoons salt

1 tablespoon sweet paprika

4 – 6 tablespoons powdered chile,
   New Mexico or California (NOT chile-spice blend)
   OR 6 chiles,
   California, New Mexico or pasilla
   (pulverized in electric spice mill)

1/4 cup water

1/3 cup cider vinegar

2 tablespoons port wine

Blend all the spices and the chile powder together. Add 1/4 cup water and blend into a paste. We prefer the higher amount of chile as it produces a very spicy sausage – not burning hot – and the meat will be a darker color. If you want a less picante sausage, use the lesser amount of chile powder and a bit more paprika. California chile powder is usually quite mild; New Mexico chile is very, very hot. Pasilla chile powder is a darker color with a hint of sweetness. I like to use 2 tablespoons of each chile powder. Add chile seeds if you like your chorizo hot.

Using a food processor or meat grinder, grind pork and fat in one-thirds, adding a little of the spices and garlic to each portion. To the ground meat add all the rest of the chile paste, the vinegar and wine, mixing well with your hands. If you wish to test-taste, fry a tiny patty for five minutes until done. Taste for desired seasoning. Let the finished sausage mellow in a glass bowl or crock in the refrigerator 24 hours before using. It freezes well if you do not plan to use it within a couple of days.

This homemade chorizo can be added to your paella, arroz con pollo, or albóndigon.

Our family loved to eat, and when not discussing memorable meals they had eaten or were about to eat, they were pondering over what should be prepared for the next meal. Even the men, particularly Grandpa, had opinions on how much basil or chile or whatever should be added to a dish. (I think I would have thrown him out of my kitchen for he not only offered his opinions, he was quite loudly opinionated.) Later generations of the family remember a variety of foods, greatly influenced by the Chilean background of Grandpa's father, Nicolas, and Grandmama's mother, Cecilia. Italian foods, from the numerous Italian immigrants flowing into the Santa Clara Valley, found their way into the rancho kitchens, and if the Early Californios weren't stewing doves in wine or simmering chicken in marinara sauce, they were tossing Parmesan and Romano cheeses into their California frijoles.

Many guests often happily sat down to the table at the ranch and the house in town where Grandmama and Grandpa always made another place. There were times when finances were bleak and there were many children to feed. That's when Grandmama's Chicken Wing Spaghetti Sauce became infamous - and those were the days when a clever grandma could talk the butcher into giving her free chicken wings.

GRANDMAMA'S INFAMOUS
EIGHT CHICKEN WING SPAGHETTI SAUCE TO FEED TEN PEOPLE

olive oil for sauteing

1 onion, chopped

4 cloves garlic, minced

> *(Grandmama was a great believer in the health-giving qualities of garlic)*

2 stalks celery (use some of the leaves)

3 carrots, chopped

1 small bay leaf

2 or 3 spikes of fresh rosemary

1 teaspoon dried sage

1 1/2 teaspoons dried sweet basil
    (or use 1 tablespoon if you have fresh)
5 sprigs parsley, chopped
6 dried Italian mushrooms, soaked
2 cans tomato paste
8 large, fresh tomatoes, peeled and chopped
    OR 2 large cans tomatoes
8 chicken wings
1 cup Romano cheese, freshly grated
2 pounds thin spaghetti

Saute onion, garlic and herbs in olive oil in cast iron pan. After softened, add chopped celery, carrots and parsley. Rinse the dried mushrooms and soak in a cup of hot water for 1/2 hour. Add the tomato paste and tomatoes. Saute the chicken wings in olive oil separately for about 15 minutes. Put them in the pan with the sauce. Chop the soaked mushrooms and add to the pan. Reserve the mushroom liquid and strain into the sauce by pouring through a corner of a clean tea towel. Simmer the sauce for 3 hours.

Boil spaghetti until al dente. Drain. Toss with some olive oil on a large platter and cover lavishly with Romano cheese. Smother with the marinara sauce and serve. The chicken wings flavor the sauce marvelously, but only the first served will get one. If Grandmama had more people to feed, she just added more spaghetti to the pot and grated more Romano cheese. There was always lots of good French bread and green salad with oil and vinegar dressing. This marinara sauce freezes beautifully, should you have any left over.

SPINACH SPAGHETTI

The elegant dining table would be set with all the necessary accoutrements for eating spinach spaghetti - the deep plates, forks, and the heavy soup spoons perfect for winding pasta. Knives were unnecessary. A one pound hunk of the finest Parmigiano Reggiano cheese waited by his plate along with the grater and such was the setting for the Piazzas' favorite meal. Mr. Piazza, who had long since made his fortune, doted on the peasant food remembered from his native Southern Italy. He insisted that the cheese be grated at the table and he would do it. While he waited by his cheese, sipping at the red wine, everyone dashed about the kitchen preparing the rest of the simple ingredients. Of course, in our family the patriarch's palate was equally respected so after observing her friends' ritual, Grandmama brought it home and Grandpa grated the cheese for this savory pasta.

Before serving time, assemble the following:

1 - 1/2 pounds semolina spaghetti
2 pounds fresh spinach,
washed in several changes of water
3 - 4 cloves garlic, minced
virgin olive oil
salt and freshly ground pepper
Parmesan cheese, grated

Remove most of the stems from the spinach. Steam the spinach, using only the water clinging to the leaves, for 3 minutes. Drain and spread out on a large plate so it will cool quickly. Squeeze out most of the water and save for minestrone. Chop the spinach. While the spaghetti is boiling to the al dente state (8 - 10 minutes), saute the minced garlic and chopped spinach in several tablespoons of olive oil for about 5 - 8 minutes.

Place the drained spaghetti on a large platter and put the spinach in its own bowl. Carry it all to the Honorary Cheese Grater. He should now have the spaghetti, the spinach, a cruet of olive oil, salt, pepper and the cheese. Lacking the inclination for ceremony you can do it all yourself in the kitchen. Or just grate the cheese in advance and toss everything at the table.

The spinach and a few tablespoons of olive oil should be lovingly tossed with the spaghetti. Lastly, the grated cheese and fresh pepper are added. Toss again. The cheese will stick to the green-flecked pasta and the garlicky aroma of it all is almost too much to bear. My children refuse to believe the green flecks are really spinach because it is widely known among people under ten that spinach cannot taste that good.

On the ranch, wild doves and pigeons were considered a delicacy and the men would wait until dusk when the birds would be nesting for the night, then shoot into the eucalyptus trees at the end of The Lane. If they came back with a dozen doves, a wine stew would be prepared.

DOVES IN WINE

12 doves or pigeons, cleaned and prepared for cooking
(squab are also good)
2 teaspoons dried oregano flowers
or use just oregano leaves
3 teaspoons salt
2 cloves garlic, minced
2 teaspoons dried basil leaves
olive oil
2 cups dry red wine
(may need to add more during cooking)
1 cup water

Make a paste by mashing garlic into the salt and adding the dried herbs and rub over the birds. Fry in olive oil, sprinkling with a little pepper, until golden brown on all sides. Pour the wine and water over the birds and simmer for 1 hour, covering the pan tightly. Check to see they are not sticking. Keep adding a little wine and water if the liquid evaporates. These birds were usually served with just plain rice and plenty of bread for dunking.

When tamales were made it was by the hundreds so they only appeared for festive times – two or three occasions – during the year. When the family hungered for the tamale flavor, Grandmama made pastel de tamal, one of the greatest tamale pies I have ever come upon. Later, Mama, who was the great modernist, produced a pastel de tamal with a cornmeal-cheese crust and even Grandmama admitted it was quite good, so I give you both versions. If you are a traditionalist, you will prefer the delightful masa crust, but - Mama, yours is so, so good, too.

Grandmama and Mama varied their tamale pies with what was available - a poached or fricaseed chicken or rabbit, or a beef chuck that had been simmered in meat stock and cut into chunks. More recently, they used lean ground beef. Grandmama always used fresh, green chiles in her pastel; whereas Mama, bowing to my father's Wisconsin-German heritage, deleted chiles entirely.

PASTEL DE TAMAL, TAMALE PIE

1 onion, chopped

1 clove garlic, minced

1 - 2 tablespoons oil

1 chicken, poached and meat removed from bones
  (discard skin)
    OR 2 1/2 pounds chuck roast, simmered in broth
      or seasoned water until tender
    OR 2 pounds ground round or sirloin

4 ears corn, kernels cut off
    OR 7 ounce can of corn

3 medium tomatoes, skinned and seeded, cut into pieces

1 small can tomato sauce

1 red or green bell pepper, chopped

73

4 or 5 fresh green chiles, California or Anaheim,
  flamed, peeled, seeded and chopped
  OR 4 - 5 canned green chiles, chopped
1 cup black olives, pitted
1 tablespoon chile powder
1 teaspoon crushed comino seeds
1 teaspoon oregano
1 1/2 teaspoons salt
freshly ground pepper to taste

Saute onion and garlic in hot oil until softened. If you are using ground meat, add to pan and saute until meat is browned. Otherwise, add all the rest of the vegetables and spices and, lastly, the cooked meat or chicken. Simmer for twenty minutes.

Meanwhile, prepare the crust:

MASA CHEESE CRUST

1 1/3 cups dehydrated masa harina, Quaker brand
3/4 teaspoon salt
2 teaspoons chile powder, California or New Mexico
1/2 teaspoon baking powder
2 cups (approximately) hot chicken broth
4 tablespoons oil (corn oil is best)
2/3 cup sharp Cheddar cheese, grated

Blend all dry ingredients. Do not add cheese yet. To dry mixture, slowly add broth, blending. Add oil. The mixture should be of a spreading consistency, but not so thick it will sit in dollops on top of the pastel. If too runny, add a tablespoon more masa; if not creamy enough, add a bit more broth if you have it, or water. Add the grated cheese. Using a greased 2 - 3 quart casserole, place half of the masa mixture on bottom. Put the meat filling on top and next spread the remaining masa - cheese mixture for the top crust. Since Grandmama did not have foil, she always soaked about eight dry corn husks, drained them, and laid them over the masa crust, tucking the edges of the husks down into the pot so the flavors would be sealed in. This makes a pretty, peasant dish to bring to your table especially if your casserole is of stoneware, but I have just as successfully used foil to seal my pot of pastel de tamal. Bake at 350 degrees for 50 - 60 minutes. Remove from oven and let pastel rest for 15 minutes before serving.

MAMA'S CORNMEAL CRUST

3/4 cup stoneground cornmeal
1/2 teaspoon salt
1 tablespoon butter
2 eggs, beaten
3 cups milk
1 1/2 cups sharp Cheddar cheese, grated

Blend cornmeal and 1 cup of the milk. Heat remaining 2 cups milk and the butter to boiling point. Gradually add the cornmeal mixture, stirring with whisk to avoid lumping. When well blended, cover and simmer on very low heat for 10 minutes. Add salt. Stir a little of the hot mixture (1/4 cup) into the eggs. Blend quickly then stir the egg mixture into the hot corn mush which you have removed from the fire. Stir in 1 cup of the cheese. Place half the cornmeal mixture on the bottom of a 2 - 3 quart casserole, add filling (see above recipe) and place the rest of the cornmeal on top, spreading it to the edges of dish or pan. Sprinkle with the remaining 1/2 cup grated cheese. Bake at 350 degrees for 50 minutes. Remove and allow to set for 15 minutes. Puncture the crust in a couple of places to release steam.

As a herald of late summer and autumn, corn appeared at our table. Because we could only have them for that all too brief season, green corn tamales were considered a rare delicacy which we began clamoring for in the hot days of July when the corn was still growing in the field. "When can we have green corn tamales?" "Soon, soon," Grandmama would promise. But they never came soon enough nor did we ever eat too many to tire of them before the corn was gone for another year.

The following recipe for geen corn tamales has been developed to adjust for our present-day corn, which is far juicier and less starchy than corn was in earlier days. Cornmeal is added to absorb some of the corn milk and also to make tamales of more substance. In our family, we never added green chiles or cheese because we loved the pure essence of corn and we already put chiles in enough dishes.

GREEN CORN TAMALES
(makes 10 - 12 small tamales)

10 ears fresh corn, scraped

2 tablespoons butter

1/2 cup sweet cream

1/2 teaspoon salt, or more to your taste

1 tablespoon sugar

1/2 cup stoneground cornmeal,

> *or a bit more if the resulting mixture seems runny*

1/2 teaspoon baking powder

1/4 teaspoon white pepper, freshly ground

Remove the cornhusks by trimming off the ends of the cobs so you can easily unfurl or unwind each husk separately, without tearing. Do not pull off. Put the largest husks in the sink and cover with hot water. Soak the husks while preparing the tamale dough.

Grated corn has an especially sweet, delicate flavor. Run a sharp knife down the center of each row of kernels. Once you have done this to the whole ear of corn over a bowl, you should press against the corn kernels with the dull side of a table knife. Work from top to bottom around the whole ear of corn and you will soon have the hearts of the corn kernels and their precious juices in your bowl.

Melt the butter in a nonstick frying pan, add the corn and juices, the cream, salt, sugar, and white pepper. Simmer over medium heat until the mixture thickens and some of the juices have evaporated. This process will require only from 5 - 8 minutes. Cool. Stir in the cornmeal and baking powder.

Drain the cornhusks on paper towels, patting away any excess moisture with more paper towels. To make a tamale, overlap at least three husks and place about 3 tablespoons of corn filling down the center. Fold over the sides and then the ends. Placing string under the ends, tie like a little package.

Using a steamer, or a fold-out vegetable steamer placed in a large pot, bring a couple inches of water to a boil. Be careful the water does not seep into the steamer. On the bottom of the steamer you may overlap more cornhusks to make a nice bed for the tamales. On this, place the tied tamales on end vertically. Steam for one hour on low heat. Remove and allow to rest for at least 10 minutes before serving. These are delightful served with just dollops of sour cream and nothing else to detract from their flavor.

Often in Mexico, a sweet corn pudding is served as an accompaniment to many dishes and is particularly good with pork or chicken.

CORN PUDDING

6 ears of corn, scraped
1 stick butter
1 tablespoon sugar
4 eggs, separated

1/2 teaspoon baking powder

1 cup milk or half and half

1/2 teaspoon salt

1/4 cup dry bread crumbs

3 leaves fresh sweet basil, snipped (optional)

Using a small knife, scrape kernels from cobs (see technique described under Green Corn Tamales). Cream the butter and beat in the corn, egg yolks, sugar, salt and baking powder. Stir in the milk and basil. Whip the egg whites until they form soft peaks. Fold the egg whites and the corn mixture together. Pour into a ring mold which has been greased with butter and sprinkled with the bread crumbs. Bake in a preheated 350 degree oven for 45 – 50 minutes until golden brown. When done, go around the edges of the pudding with a sharp knife and, placing a platter over the top of the mold, invert the pudding. Serve immediately.

Great steaming platters of corn on the cob always made the children happy and once in a while we were allowed to gorge on five or six ears with no fear of having to eat our meat or vegetables or anything else that was supposed to make us nobly healthy. Grandpa liked his corn cut off the cob and fried, but we were only required to eat it this way when we were missing some teeth. Below is a lovely way of eating fresh corn – when you are beyond keeping score as to how many ears you can put away.

FRIED GREEN CORN

6 ears fresh corn
butter
1 green pepper, chopped
1 red pepper, chopped
2 tomatoes, skinned, seeded and chopped
1/3 to 1/2 cup milk
salt and black pepper to taste

Cut corn kernels from cob. Set aside. Melt butter in frying pan and saute green and red pepper until softened. Add tomatoes, corn and the smaller amount of milk, simmering for about 10 to 15 minutes. Stir frequently if the mixture seems to be sticking. Add a bit more milk if necessary. Add more butter if you wish a richer taste. Season with salt and pepper.

Sometimes when I'm hungry for the pure, sweet taste of corn, I'll fry the cut corn briefly in a couple of tablespoons of butter, and simmer with a little cream for 10 minutes.

In summer and early fall when corn, squash and tomatoes were at their peak, Grandmama made pots of colache. She always insisted the vegetables, except the corn, be sauteed in hot olive oil first before they were simmered.

COLACHE

4 tablespoons olive oil

2 medium onions, chopped

1 - 2 cloves garlic, minced

2 - 2 1/2 pounds zucchini, sliced thickly

2 tomatoes, peeled, seeded, chopped

3 or 4 ears sweet corn cut into 3 inch pieces

6 leaves fresh, sweet basil, snipped

    OR 1 teaspoon dry basil

salt and freshly ground pepper

a handful of Romano or Parmesan cheese

Saute onions and garlic in olive oil until golden (about 10 minutes). Push aside in pot and add zucchini slices and herbs. Saute for 10 minutes. Add tomatoes, salt and pepper. Cover and simmer slowly about 45 minutes, checking frequently to make sure the mixture is not sticking or becoming too dry. Stir in the cheese and place the pieces of corn within the vegetables. Cook for 15 more minutes. (Serves 4.)

Depending upon the timing of late winter rains, spring might come to the foothills of the ranch by February or early March, heralding the first mustard with its tender leaves. Of all the wild things that grew in the hills, Grandmama cherished mustard the most and she would often fry some in olive oil and garlic and eat it for her lunch along with a chunk of bread.

The potency of mustard was so admired that after pots of the greens were cooked, the liquid was drained and bottled. All the children were lined up and given their dose of mustard water as a spring tonic. Eight year old Jack thought he had a way of convincing Aunt Nicolassa the green water was dangerous and after his first spoonful of the draught, he burst through the doors, ran in circles screaming, collapsing in a heap with his eyes bugged out and mouth gaping open. Everyone else had a good laugh, but Aunt Nicolassa was waiting at the door with the next spoonful.

MOSTAZA or WILD MUSTARD GREENS

1 1/2 - 2 pounds greens, wild mustard
        or part spinach, stems removed
water
3 tablespoons olive oil
2 cloves garlic, minced
1/2 onion, minced
salt and freshly ground pepper to taste

Wash greens thoroughly in cold water. Remove the tough stalks. Steam for 15 - 20 minutes or until tender. Drain and cool. Mustard greens have a definite taste of their own. They are quite delicious chopped with fresh spinach. Chop the greens when cool, combining them with steamed spinach (steam for only 5 minutes) if you like. Heat oil in heavy skillet, sauteing onion and garlic until softened. Add greens and saute for another 5 minutes to blend flavors. Sometimes on the ranch they would stir these sauteed greens into frijoles.

The mission fathers had spread mustard seeds from one end of California to the other to mark the trails between missions, but in some areas such as the lush Santa Clara Valley, the mustard grew into such a jungle it became a convenient hiding place for banditos and horse thieves. Eventually, the scourge of mustard was dealt with by the Chinese who came along and made mustard paste for a condiment which turned out to be quite profitable. The governor and all the town officials were amazed they had not thought of making table mustard, but the families on the ranchos continued to eat their greens and make the children drink the annual spring tonic.

Another vegetable that grew untamed in neglected fields was my favorite, and still is when I can find it. Fava beans, known commonly in California as horsebeans, grew in early spring and disappeared with the heat. Fava beans, now considered an exotic vegetable in American markets, are becoming increasingly available so you do not have to forage in the fields. Always choose the smaller and narrower pods as they will contain the tenderest beans.

HORSEBEANS

1 pound shelled horsebeans
   (if the beans are large and mealy, peel off the outer
   covering and use the smaller bean inside - a tip from
   my Chinese groceryman)

olive oil (no substitute)

wine vinegar

1 clove garlic, minced

2 green onions, minced

1/4 cup cilantro, minced

Remove the horsebeans from their long pods. If the beans are small you will not need to remove the outer covering. Simmer in a couple of inches of boiling water for about 10 minutes. Check by biting into one because the beans are quite grainy if underdone. Drain. While horsebeans are warm, dress with the olive oil and wine vinegar to your taste. Add the minced garlic, onion and cilantro. Season with salt or garlic salt. Serve as a salad course.

Olive oil was always used on the ranch instead of butter or lard, and vegetables were not only dressed with it for cold salads, but were also stewed with fragrant green olive oil which was pressed right on the premises. String beans were cooked much like the vegetables for colache.

STRING BEANS OR EJOTES

1 1/2 - 2 pounds string beans

3 tablespoons olive oil

1 onion, minced

1 clove garlic

2 ripe tomatoes, peeled, seeded and chopped

2 teaspoons wine vinegar
salt
freshly ground pepper to taste
parsley, minced

Purchase or pick from your own garden the smallest, narrowest string beans as they will be the most tender. The Chinese long beans now more increasingly available are great for this dish. String the beans. If they are older, French cut them and they will be more tender.

Heat olive oil in a pan you can cover. Saute the onion and garlic until softened then add the minced tomatoes and green beans. Cover and simmer for 10 - 15 minutes or until tender. Remove lid and cook a bit longer to reduce any watery liquid in the bottom. During the last few minutes add the seasoning and vinegar.

It was an old Indian belief that eating squash blossoms brought fertility. Some of the Spaniards on the ranchos, during the peak autumn season of pumpkins, ate blossoms because they savored them, and it was not uncommon to find fifteen children at many family tables in those days.

Grandmama would occasionally chop some pumpkin blossoms into her vegetable soup to add to its volume, but it was Mama who made up a light, airy beer batter in which to dip the whole blossom then fry it in hot fat. She would also skin pieces of chicken or rabbit and use this batter for frying. The chicken must first be dusted with flour so the batter will stick. Golden chicken done in this manner will delight everyone.

BLOSSOM FRITTERS

Select a dozen male squash or pumpkin blossoms from your garden. Do this in the morning, because as the day warms the flowers begin to close. The male blossoms grow at the tip of narrow stems. When you pick, leave some stem attached so you may place them in a jar of water as you would a bouquet. Sprinkle or spray them with a mist of water and pat dry. Before cooking, trim off the stem and remove the stamens.

Batter

3/4 cup flour
1/4 teaspoon salt
2 eggs, separated
1 tablespoon oil
3/4 cup warm, flat beer

Beat the yolks with beer, salt and flour until well blended. Allow this mixture to stand at room temperature for 1 - 2 hours. Before using, whip egg whites until stiff, but not dry and grainy. Fold gently into the batter.

Fill the blossoms with a little mild, white cheese such as Monterey Jack, twist the tips of the flowers to close the ends; dip in batter to coat; fry in hot oil; drain on paper towels. Serve while warm.

For all the elaborate preparations and conversation we centered on food, sometimes we craved a simple and comforting meal that took only minutes to prepare. Potatoes were never eaten alone, but were chopped into cubes and stirred up with chopped beef and chile or mixed into a spicy picadillo or an omelet. Grandmama always seemed to have a couple of parboiled potatoes in the icebox.

POTATO OMELET

2 Russet potatoes, cooked in their jackets until tender
1/2 onion, chopped
1/2 bell pepper, chopped
1/2 teaspoon salt
freshly ground pepper
5 eggs
olive oil
sharp Cheddar cheese or Parmesan, grated
    (about 3 tablespoons)

Remove the skins of the potatoes (or leave them on if you prefer, as I often do) and cut into cubes. Saute the onion, bell pepper and potato cubes in a little olive oil for about 10 minutes until lightly browned. Whisk the eggs, salt and pepper and pour over the top of the potato mixture. Cook on low heat, shaking pan until eggs are set. This omelet was also made with a little fried chorizo or diced ham tossed into the potatoes. Sprinkle the surface of the omelet with the cheese and place under hot broiler until cheese melts. Scatter minced parsley over the finished omelet and cut into wedges to serve.

My mother made friends with the Watkins man who drove around in his little truck filled with the spicy smells, and from him we purchased superb vanilla and cinnamon. This gentle Louisiana man and Mama talked food, exchanging recipes. One of the gems he gave us was his Mama's Fried Okra and when it was prepared for a rancho barbeque it was as popular as watermelon. And that's popular.

THE WATKIN'S MAN'S MAMA'S FRIED YOUNG OKRA

Slice the tiniest, young okra you can find (preferably should be no longer than 1 1/2 inches and squeak when pinched) into quarter inch slices, lengthwise. Roll generously in stone-ground cornmeal. Slice three or four ripe tomatoes and roll in the same cornmeal. Slice a fat, red onion and saute in a little oil in a cast iron pan. Add a layer of okra and next the tomatoes and saute until golden. Turn over like a large pancake and saute the other side until golden. You may have to add a couple tablespoons more oil to the pan. This is a marvelous combination of vegetables, dearly loved even by those of us who do not come from Louisiana.

The use of olive oil is as necessary to true Early California cooking as the use of pure lard in Mexican cuisine. All the missions and later, most of the ranchos pressed their own olive oil and to equate this today, we must seek out the virgin, liquid green gold from Spain, Italy and France. There are many olive oils on the market which are no better than the most bleached-out vegetable oils, and there are some so heavy and coarse they would dominate any other flavor. Your search for the pure olive oil that suits your needs and taste will be well worth the extra effort.

Below is a recipe found in the archives of old Mission Santa Barbara describing the ancient way olive oil was made in Early California.

OLIVE OIL

Spread olives upon mat and leave them until wrink-led from ripeness. Crush them thoroughly in the mortars used by old women. Place olives in a large kettle. Add water to give olives the consistency of atole paste. After boiling thoroughly, take part of the olives and put into a rough sack or coarse cloth, allowing the oil to pass through. Tie the sack well and press it into a large dish of hot water. Add hot water to the olive dough many times until nothing but pure water passes through. When an olive press is not available, press the sack between the boards of a carpenter's press. After the juice has been crushed from the olives, place it upon the fire with water and boil moderately. With a ladle, skim into an earthen pot, all of the oil, which will rise to the surface. To make very pure, pour oil into a spotless kettle with a lot of hot water. The dregs will sink to the bottom. The olive oil will rise to the surface of the water.

Described above is the primitive method for extracting the virgin or first-pressed oil. Cheap olive oil is simply a product of second and third pressings of the olives made possible by modern technology – but with a result barely reminiscent of olives.

The task of pressing olive oil was dispensed with once it could be purchased from those who made it their business, but on the ranch green olives were cured in oak barrels until the place was put up for sale.

There were certain rules associated with getting into the olive barrel. One never, never reached into the barrel to get an

90

olive with the fingers. The wooden ladle hanging on the side was to be used as a dipper. Fingers could make a whole barrel of olives go bad and a horrible scum would gather on the surface as evidence someone had done the unmentionable. Olives were never canned, but always left in the curing barrels.

CURED GREEN OLIVES

Pick enough full-size green olives from a nearby tree to fill half your container - a crockery or stoneware vessel (do not use a metal or plastic container). This will allow room for the curing liquid. Do not pick black olives as they will be wrinkly and soft when cured. The best for curing are the Sevillano or Manzanillo varieties. Most of the ranches had their own olive trees and these silvery-green trees are still common in many areas of the West.

Cover the olives completely with the following lye solution:

Mix 2 1/2 ounces concentrated lye (caustic soda purchased at a pharmacy) with 1 gallon of water. Do your mixing and pouring carefully and do not allow the solution to come in contact with your skin as it will burn. The function of the lye solution is to remove the natural bitter taste of the green olives. You cannot eat green olives directly off the tree because of this bitterness.

After approximately 8 hours, begin checking for penetration of the lye by cutting into the olive. Wash the olive in cold water before checking so you do not get the solution on your hands. The lye should penetrate 3/4 of the way to the olive pit, indicated by a color change. Soak the olives a couple of hours longer if penetration is not adequate.

Drain off all the lye solution and add fresh, cold water to the crock. Each day for seven days, drain off the water and replace with fresh. It also helps if you change the water a couple of times during the day.

After this seven day period the olives are ready to be cured in a brine consisting of 1 pound sea salt or rock salt (do not use bleached table salt) to 1 gallon of water. On the ranch the olives were always placed in an oak barrel, but you may use a crock, keg or stoneware vessel. Again, do not use metal or plastic. Place the drained olives and the salt solution inside your chosen container and cover well so it is sealed against insects and dust particles as most probably you will find it necessary to keep your container outside or in some cool, out-of-the-way spot. The olives should be allowed to cure for a couple of months, but a sampling can be permitted at an earlier time - if the ladle is used instead of fingers. Since the brine is quite salty, you may wish to wash it off the olives with cold water before enjoying this delicacy.

PICKLED PIG'S FEET

There were lazy Saturday afternoons spent around Grandmama's kitchen table with friends, cronies and the loyal sons coming to pay a call on Mama and Papa. Of course, Grandmama would be well-supplied with all the foods her daughters-in-law avoided preparing for their husbands - chicharrones (fried pork skins) and pickled pig's feet. The table would be laden with onion eggs, dry salami, freshly made chicharrones, both the dark, bitter olives and the green ranch olives, hunks of crusty bread, and the pinkish morsels I loved in blind imitation of my uncles. Something called "pig's feet" in a slur of the tongue. One day I asked them and they said, "Yes, yes, they are really pig's feet." The pink, vinegary morsels never tasted the same again, but this volume would not be complete without Grandmama's recipe for them.

3 young and tender pig's feet

1 teaspoon salt

2 bay leaves

1 teaspoon dry mustard

1 teaspoon mace

8 whole cloves

1 whole dried red pepper

2 teaspoons salt

1 teaspoon fine pepper

1/2 teaspoon cayenne pepper

1 pint apple cider vinegar

Clean the pig's feet by scraping with a small, sharp knife. Soak in several changes of cold water. Split and crack the feet in several places (or ask the butcher to do it) so that you will have pieces small enough to fit into a crock or glass jar.

Place the pig's feet in a pot and cover with cold water. Bring to a boil and drain. Cover with more cold water and 1 teaspoon of salt and bring to a boil. Turn the heat down and simmer for 4 hours or until tender. Drain off all liquid.

Boil the rest of the ingredients together and pour with the hot, spicy vinegar over the pig's feet which you have placed into a glass bowl, large jar or crock. Cover and let them marinate for at least 1 day before eating. Keep refrigerated.

An engraving of the old California custom of sun-drying red chiles strung on crossbeams.

CHAPTER IV

CHILE, STAPLE OF THE RANCHO KITCHEN

he original settlement of California was the un-rivaled civilizing center for a coastline stretching a thousand miles. At the heart of the early cuisine were chiles, part of the culinary treasure borrowed from the ancient Indian culture of Mexico. They simply could not live without chiles and so chiles found their way into many dishes. Chiles made the rangy beef cattle which fed on the wild fodder in the hills taste more palatable, and when spicy sausage, known as chorizo, was made from pork, chiles were the dominant seasoning.

On the self-sustaining ranchos an indispensable part of the diet was beef, especially in the form of carne seca (jerky) which was preserved for months in its coating of chile. When carne seca was needed for a meal it was pounded in a mortar, put in a pan with a little hot lard and water, red chile, tomato with a minced onion and potato. Carne seca was also just boiled in plain water if the cook was in a hurry. Perhaps it was from such a taste of boiled jerky that prompted one visiting Parisian to state that the culinary arts were but slightly developed in mid-nineteenth century California.

Although chiles were the mainstay of this wilderness diet in Early California, foods advanced, thankfully, away from wild greens, carne seca and chile on everything; but the red chile puree remained a staple in all rancho kitchens to be kept on hand for making sauces, enchiladas, carne con chile, beef tamales and other traditional foods. When my kitchen is pungently filled with the smell of chiles being soaked and pureed, I recall Grandmama's and Mama's cooking and, admittedly, chiles are the Proustian madelaines taking me back to an old kitchen where I stood at a counter and watched hands push dark, red mush through a conical sieve. Many of the traditional dishes require various types of the red, dried chiles and you must familiarize yourself with some of those most frequently used so you are not at the complete mercy of their whimsical identification in the different ethnic areas of the United States.

DISTINGUISHING TYPES OF DRIED RED CHILES

CALIFORNIA or ANAHEIM

Pale red with a smooth, shiny skin. Considered mild by chile aficionados. Strains of this chile have been grown in California since the arrival of the early settlers and mission fathers. These long, pointed chiles, popularly known as "red chiles", are the dried version of the green California or anaheim.

NEW MEXICO

Refers to a chile type grown in New Mexico but similar to the anaheim or California chile, except it is hotter. It is difficult to distinguish between the California and New Mexico chile, but the New Mexico seems to have a more brittle, papery skin. For use in their native cooking, Mexicans living in the United States prefer this chile to the milder anaheim.

ANCHO or PASILLA

Deep red-brown with a wrinkled, dusty appearance. These are the dried version of the poblano chiles, known in California as the pasilla chiles. Mild to medium picante. They may also be called pasilla anchos in some markets. It is the most commonly used in Mexican cookery. I like to use half anchos and half California chiles for enchilada sauce as the anchos are meatier and add richness and body. If you prefer a hotter, richer sauce, use a higher percentage of anchos or pasillas.

JAPONÉS

These are the ripened, dried serrano chiles. Very hot. To be used as an accent in sauces as is frequently done by the Italians and Chinese. If a sauce is not hot enough for your taste, add a japonés chile or the piquines eaten like peanuts by Texas cowboys.

PASILLA NEGRO or PASILLA

About 6 inches long and 1 inch wide. These chiles are long, slender and almost black, giving the characteristic, almost black ochre color to traditional mole poblano of Mexico. Be aware it may also be called the pasilla, just as the ancho chile may be called the pasilla.

MULATO

This chile is the same shape as the pasilla ancho and it is difficult to tell them apart unless they are side by side, but the mulato is the darker brown, rather than the dark red of the pasilla ancho. The ancho, in comparison, appears the more wrinkled of the two similar types. The mulato can have a faintly sweet flavor. This chile is not widely available in the

United States except in Mexican markets where it is sought out for use in preparing mole poblano.

RED CHILE PUREE, THE RANCHO STAPLE

In the old days, chiles were either soaked in hot water and the flesh then scraped from the translucent skin with a sharp knife, or as Grandmama did it, the soaked chiles were pushed through a sieve so the result would be a velvety puree without any irritating bits of skin. The modern blender eliminates this task, and I believe the miniscule bits of chile serve to make a thick sauce and provide chile bran helping to supplement an altogether too refined modern diet.

10 red California or Anaheim chiles, dried
6 pasilla chiles, dried
   (optional, but adds richness to the final sauce)
1 clove garlic
boiling water

Remove stems, seeds and veins from chiles, holding under cool running water to rinse well. Break the chiles into pieces, making sure the pieces are well rinsed and free of dust and grit. Place chiles in large bowl and cover with boiling water. Add the peeled clove of garlic. Allow to soak at least one hour or more. Place 1/3 of the chiles into a blender jar (not a food processor) adding a little of the soaking liquid which you, of course, have not yet thrown away. Blend into a smooth puree adding chile liquid only as necessary so the sauce does not become watery. Continue to puree in batches, adding only 1/4 cup liquid at a time so you maintain a heavy sauce consistency. Place the chile puree in a clean, glass jar and store in the refrigerator where it will keep about a week. It also freezes well. Makes about 1 quart red chile puree. Reserve for making red enchiladas, chile colorado, carne con chile, or sopa de albondigas.

FRESH GREEN CHILES

Fresh chiles are simply the green, unripened version of red chiles. They are available in many places, particularly the western and southwestern United States throughout the year although the proper season runs from July to October.

When you purchase fresh chiles, choose those which are not convoluted, dented or of an unusual shape as these chiles will not flame easily or evenly, and crooked chiles are difficult to fill if that is what you want to do. Undersized chiles are often immature and will lack flavor nor will they have much vitamin content.

Fresh, green chiles will keep a couple of weeks in the refrigerator if kept dry from the moisture of other vegetables.

Wrap them in a dry towel or paper towels, rather than plastic bags which are ruinous to many fresh vegetables. Keep checking the stored chiles for any spoilage as one bad chile can spoil the lot.

DISTINGUISHING THE TYPES OF GREEN CHILES

The chiles listed below are simply those most available and those favored for the recipes in this book. I have purposely not strayed into a compendium of rare, exotic types or the hybrids increasingly available.

ANAHEIM OR CALIFORNIA

The most widely available chile in the West no longer has to be searched for in ethnic markets as it has found its way into many a supermarket. This is the chile seared and canned by Ortega in the California coastal city of Oxnard. In the canned form it is fine as a seasoning, but it will not give you the texture needed when you want to prepare chile rellenos. When buying a fresh chile pepper, look for shiny, bright skin that is smooth and unwrinkled. Wrinkled skin means old chiles. Fresh chiles should feel firm with no soft spots. This chile seems to be getting milder and milder, and I wonder if agricultural science is breeding chiles which will not burn. Anaheims are mild on the scale of chiles.

POBLANO OR PASILLA

These chiles are dark green, shorter and broader than the Anaheim. This is my favorite chile because of the rich, picante flavor and the ideal shape for stuffing. It is the most commonly used chile in northern and central Mexico and is now found fresh in Mexican markets in California and the Southwest.

JALAPEÑO

Short, plump and dark green. Hot. Used most frequently in sauces and is especially savory blended with tomatillos (green husk tomatoes) and cilantro for a green sauce. Jalapeños are found fresh in many supermarkets in the West and Southwest and the Hispanic markets of large cities. The canned, pickled ones, labeled "en escabeche" are nibbled on for appetizers in Mexico. Soaked or canned jalapeños are delicious stuffed with something creamy like cream cheese, minced onion and crabmeat. Often they are labeled simply "hot peppers."

CHIPOTLE

The dried, smoked jalapeño chile. In the United States it is available canned and only to be found in Mexican stores. You will usually find six or seven chiles to the six ounce can. The chipotle is used to flavor broth, stews and chicken or turkey. Very hot with a delightful smoky flavor.

Slim, very dark green and very hot. Serranos are true to the maxim, "the smaller the chile, the hotter the chile." Mexicans like to put minced serranos into scrambled eggs or in the salsa for huevos rancheros. Serranos are for chile aficionados and those with conditioned palates. Sparingly used as a seasoning, this chile will give a lift to your sauces. If you cannot find the serrano, substitute the jalapeño, fresh or canned.

ROASTING CHILES FOR COOKING

Chiles have a tough, translucent skin which must be removed before eating them in their fresh state. Listed below are several techniques for blistering so the skin may be easily peeled off.

When they saw a man going anywhere in a big hurry, the Early Californians often commented, ' *"Parece que aquel amigo dejo chiles tatemando,"* or "It looks like that man left some chiles roasting." You must pay heed when roasting chiles.

FLAME METHOD: This is my favorite method as the quick surface flame leaves the chile's flesh crisp and imparts a marvelous smoky flavor. Holding the chile by its stem keep turning it over the open flame of a gas stove until the chile's surface is charred. Most novices flame the chile too little and then cannot remove the skin. As each chile is charred, wrap in a damp towel which will steam the skin to make it easier to remove. Next, plunge the chiles into ice water to stop further cooking from contained heat. When I do not have much time, I flame the chiles and immediately rinse off charred skin by holding under running water.

BROILER METHOD: Preheat broiler and place rack in highest position. Place chiles on a cookie sheet that can be easily removed so you may keep turning the chiles until they are sufficiently charred. Using this method the chiles will become more cooked by the intense heat of the broiler. This system is faster than flaming each chile individually and is a good one to use when you are preparing a group of chiles for a dish other than chiles rellenos which require a crisper texture. When using this technique, after removing the chiles from the broiler, place them in ice water to immediately stop the cooking.

HOT OIL METHOD: This method does not imbue the chiles with that rustic, smoky flavor although the chiles remain pleasingly firm and bright green. You will need to place at least 2 inches of oil in a heavy skillet and heat to almost smoking. Poke a tiny hole in the side of each chile (in the spot where you will later slit it to remove the seeds) to prevent exploding when the chile is placed in the hot oil. It is recommended that the chiles not be ice cold from the refrigerator. Blot off any surface moisture with a paper towel. Place one or two chiles at a time into the hot oil. Turn once and remove as soon as the translucent skin loosens. Wrap the chiles in several thicknesses of paper towel and place in a plastic bag so they may steam. This method is not worth the trouble and mess if you are preparing less than six chiles, but I do prefer the hot oil if I need pasillas for chiles rellenos and do not have a flame available.

ELECTRIC BURNER METHOD: Take your stainless steel rack used for cooling cakes and place it over an electric burner; turn heat to high. Put the chiles directly on the grid of the cake rack (it will hold about three chiles). Keep turning them while they char evenly. The process will take about two minutes. Put them in a plastic bag to steam for two to three minutes to loosen the skin and it will slip off easily.   Unlike the broiler method, this process will not cook the chile, just char it properly. A fast method for doing more than one chile at a time.

ALTERNATIVE METHODS OF CHARRING: Purchase a small propane torch such as those sold in hardware stores and spread your chiles en masse over a baking sheet to torchflame them.   Work in an open, safe area of your kitchen or patio.   Do not work near curtains or other highly flammable material. The advantage to this method is that it is relatively fast and chars the chiles without cooking them.   I can only recommend whichever way works best for your style, but the supreme method still remains the open flame of a gas burner stove.

If you wish your chiles to be more crisp, you may skip wrapping them in a towel or plastic bag after the blistering step. Lay the chiles out on the kitchen counter to cool or transfer to plastic bag and place in freezer for 15 minutes. If I have the occasion to buy a case of fresh chiles in the fall, I blister them and freeze the ones I am not using immediately. The charred skin is easier to slip off after freezing and saves dealing with too many chiles at one time.

PEELING AND SEEDING CHILES

After you have blistered the chiles and either cooled or wrapped them for further steaming, you are ready to remove the seeds and skins. First peel off the loosened skin, rinsing the chiles under running cool water. Do not worry if a few stubborn pieces of skin remain as this will not affect the texture or flavor. If you plan to use the chiles for stuffing, be extra cautious in handling so as not to break the steamed flesh. Slit open one side of the chile and carefully pull out the seeds from the dangling seedpod. Often if you try to pull out the veins the flesh will tear. Remove all of the seeds by rinsing inside the chile with cold water. Hot water will release the fumes of the capsaicin oil. Some instructions for working with chiles suggest using rubber gloves so the volatile oils do not get on your fingers. I find working with gloves cumbersome so I wash my hands in warm, soapy water brushing my fingers with a soft vegetable brush to remove the oils, and I am careful not to stick my finger in my eye or anywhere on my face after cleaning chiles.

REMOVING THE HEAT FROM CHILES

There is a myth that the heat of chiles is concentrated in the seeds. The heat is really inside the little blisters found along the yellow streak on the veins that run from the chile's cap (also hot because in the preparation much of the capsaicin oil is released in the cap) to the tip. Usually, when the chile is being prepared for eating, the little blisters are broken, releasing their oils upon the seeds and veins. Therein lies the myth about hot seeds. It is quite difficult to remove the yellow streak on the vein (near the seed heart) without actually cutting it out – which is no solution if you want the chile intact. However, if you are preparing salsas or stews you may easily cut between the veins to remove the section with the hot yellowish streak and then cut your chile into strips or chop it. Beware if you see an orange rather than yellow streak, for this chile will be particularly hot. Because much of the capsaicin oil escapes into the chile's cap, you may cut off the cap and discard. These procedures are only to be followed if you fear picante food or you are cooking for vulnerable friends.

A procedure followed in Mexico for diminishing the heat of chiles is to soak them in a warm water bath. Place 1 tablespoon sea salt, 1/4 cup vinegar to 1 & 1/2 quarts of warm water and leave the peeled, seeded chiles to soak. My maid, Pueblito, would smell the soaking water after ten minutes and if the fumes made her eyes smart she would drain off the water and start again with fresh water, salt and vinegar, soaking the chiles for another ten minutes. However, be cautioned that the warm water reduces heat, but does not eliminate it. After soaking, a fiery chile may become a hot chile, and a hot chile may become a slightly picante chile. Dry the chiles well and, if they are not to be used immediately, store them in plastic bags for up to two days or freeze them. The moisture will keep them from sticking to one another and you can pull out one or two from the freezer as you need them.

Chiles found on the same plant can vary in hotness so you can commonly buy a dozen fresh pasilla chiles to discover that half of them are very picante (hot) and half are mild as bell peppers.

The intensity of Mexican chiles is sometimes attributed to the volcanic soil, but I have tasted searing chiles plucked from the rich loam of the San Joaquin Valley in California. The general rule is that cool climates with damp soil are least likely to produce incendiary chiles. But since the weather varies from year to year, the nuances of climate can differentiate chiles just as grapes vary from Bordeaux to the hillsides of the Cote d'Or. It is this mystique of chiles, *las malaguetas* or the grains of paradise as they are known in Mexico – their insouciance – which encourages my affair with them to the degree that when I travel I always have with me a couple of jars of picante sauce to keep my celestial bearings, and I know I am addicted beyond the ancestral calling of my forbears at Rancho Los Tularcitos. In fact, my grandmother, who always ate lightly, would be shocked at the idea of her granddaughter gorging on chiles.

SAUTEED GREEN CHILES WITH CHEESE

My husband and I have often dined on a platter of these golden chiles with frosty Mexican beer and that is happiness.

8 Anaheim or California fresh chiles, prepared for cooking
sharp cheese (3 tablespoons per chile) grated
stale bread crumbs,
finely ground in blender or food processor
flour
2 whole eggs beaten with 1 tablespoons milk
butter and oil

Fill the chiles with grated cheese. Dust with flour. Dip in egg and milk. Roll generously in bread crumbs. Saute them in a sizzling mixture of butter and oil. Cook only long enough to brown the crumb batter and melt the cheese. Place in 325 degree oven to keep warm while you finish sauteing (or frying) the rest of the chiles. These are so delicious they have come to replace the classic chiles rellenos in our household because they are faster and do not seem to absorb as much oil as does the light egg batter typically used for chiles rellenos. In extravagant moments, I have used leftover brioche crumbs for the coating and then these chiles can no longer be called peasant fare.

CHILE APPETIZER

1 can of jalapeño chiles (remove seeds)

1 3 ounce package cream cheese, room temperature

1 tablespoon sour cream

1 tablespoon minced onion

1/4 cup shredded crabmeat

   OR fresh shrimp, minced

   OR water-packed albacore tuna

Remove seeds from the chiles and rinse. Mash the sour cream and cream cheese together, adding a bit more sour cream if necessary. Blend in the onion and crab or shrimp. Neatly fill each chile with the mixture. Place in hot oven for 10 minutes or until filling has been heated and is lightly puffed.

This same filling is wonderful inside mushroom caps which have been wiped clean with a paper towel. Fill the mushroom caps, but do not bake more than 8 minutes or they will begin to exude liquid and collapse because of the overcooking.

Green chiles were often preserved in brine like pickles so they could be enjoyed past the summer and fall months when they were harvested. Although there is little need for stoneware crocks and brine to preserve chiles anymore, I have found that an overnight soak or several days in brine makes another perfect chile appetizer to be eaten with sharp cheese and bread.

CHILES IN BRINE

8 California or pasilla fresh chiles
1 quart of water
1/4 cup sea salt
1 cup cider vinegar
2 cloves garlic, smashed

Flame, peel and seed chiles. Place in glass bowl or crock. Bring the brine ingredients to a simmer and immediately pour hot brine over the chiles. Soak for a week before serving. These chiles can be stored in a jar in the refrigerator for several months. Cut chiles in strips and use with cheese as an appetizer or serve in tostados, burritos and salsas.

Canned chiles are quite acceptable for many dishes with the exception of any type of chiles rellenos or stuffed chile where the earthy pungency and texture of fresh chiles are requisite. Each chile is an individual, some hot, some mild and some perfect to your taste. A good telltale sign of piquancy is to watch how many watering eyes and sniffling noses you have around the house while you are preparing chiles. One landlord we had in Mexico had a particularly elegant colonial house, always bustling with braided servant girls from the outlying rancheros. As I would stand in the luminous, tiled entry hall waiting to deliver my rent money to the senora, my eyes would water and burn and I would have the overwhelming urge to choke from the chile fumes floating down the stately halls. Someone was always flaming chiles. I had visions of a dungeon-type kitchen lined with Indian girls passing serrano chiles over flaming grates while the senor and senora sat at a long table devouring mounds of green fire.

Our maid, Pueblito, schooled me in the art of chiles. If they were too hot – a fact she would determine by smelling the soaking liquid – she would save them for herself. Pueblito's chile rellenos were always filled with the natural, sharp Mennonite cheese from Chihuahua and were so huge, each chile required an entire dinner plate all to itself – to the joy and astonishment of our guests from the States.

PUEBLITO'S CLASSIC CHILE RELLENOS CON QUESO

8 poblano or pasilla chiles
1 1/2 - 2 pounds grated sharp cheese
   (domestic Greek Kasseri, Teleme, Italian Fontina or
   sharp Cheddar)
8 large eggs, separated
   (The extra eggs simply add more volume of whipped
   batter to the proportion of liquid at the bottom.)
1/2 teaspoon salt
1/4 cup flour

peanut oil for frying
waxed paper with 1/2 cup flour
electric frying pan

Flame chiles over gas flame or sear in hot oil according to directions given earlier in chapter. As the skin is seared, wrap chiles in a heavy brown bag. Once you have seared all of your chiles and left them to steam in the bag for a few minutes, remove the skin. Make a slit in the sides and carefully remove the seeds. Be careful not to tear the flesh or the filling will leak out. Dry chiles well and stuff. I prefer using grated cheese so I may fit bits of cheese into every crevice. Dust each chile with flour and pat off excess. The hot oil should be heating in the pan. Whip the egg whites until soft peaks form adding the salt. Using the same whisk in another bowl, beat the egg yolks with the 1/4 cup flour until thick and blended. Fold the yolk mixture into the whipped egg whites. Using a wide spatula, place the chile into the egg batter, coating it well. Place coated chile on a small plate and slip into the hot oil, spooning oil over the surface of the chile. Fry until golden brown on both sides, turning once. Drain on paper towels. Keep warm on a platter in a 250 degree oven. Pueblito served these chiles without sauce or you may use the sauce below. Chiles rellenos can be made several hours ahead of time and reheated. Leftovers are good to fill omelets or to stuff into burritos along with beans.

In some parts of Mexico during a feast, fried chiles rellenos are piled high on a platter to be eaten unadorned. In another place, another time, chiles can be found floating lazily in a thin tomato broth. You must choose the way you prefer them and here is a sauce recipe:

SALSA DE TOMATES PARA CHILES RELLENOS

2 tablespoons oil

4 large tomatoes, peeled, seeded, chopped

2 green onions

1 stalk celery, chopped

1 clove garlic, minced

2 tablespoons parsley, minced

1/2 teaspoon oregano

1 cup chicken broth

1/2 teaspoon salt

pepper, freshly ground

Saute garlic, onions and celery until softened. Add tomatoes and broth. Simmer for 20 minutes. This will not be a thick salsa. Place the salsa in a large shallow baking dish and arrange the chiles in it. You'll have enough sauce for 4 - 6 stuffed chiles. If the chiles have cooled, place dish in 350 degree oven to heat and they will repuff a bit.

If you have leftover pot roast, it is only natural that you plan to make a spicy picadillo to stuff into some fresh, green poblano chiles. When we tired of chiles filled with cheese, we hungered for these.

CHILES CON PICADILLO

6 - 8 large, green poblano chiles (or pasillas)

Flame or sear the chiles, remove the skins and seeds. Dry well and set aside while preparing filling.

Picadillo

1 1/2 cups leftover pot roast
or braised beef, roughly chopped
broth
2 tablespoons oil
1 clove garlic, minced
1 medium onion, minced
2 tomatoes, peeled, seeded, chopped
1 dried chile, California or pasilla
(soak the chile in hot water for 30 minutes and puree in blender with some of the soaking liquid)
1 potato, cooked and cubed
1 carrot, cooked and cubed
1/4 cup blanched almonds, toasted lightly and chopped
1/4 cup raisins, plumped in hot water
salt to taste

Saute the onion and garlic in oil until softened. Add the tomatoes and cook until a bit thickened. Next add the chopped meat, the chile puree, the potatoes, carrot, almonds, raisins and salt. If the mixture seems dry, add some of the beef broth.

Batter for Chiles:

8 large eggs, separated
1/2 teaspoon salt
1/4 cup flour
oil for frying
        (sunflower or safflower is best)
waxed paper with 1/2 cup flour
deep, heavy skillet or electric frying pan

Fill the chiles with meat picadillo. Hold them over waxed paper and dust with flour, patting off excess. Set aside while you prepare the egg batter. Whip the egg whites until they form soft peaks. Add salt. Using the same whisk, beat the egg yolks until thickened. Stir in the flour. Fold the yolk mixture into the egg whites until well blended. Dip the filled chile into the batter to coat. Place chile on a small dessert plate and slide it into the hot oil, spooning oil over the top surface of the chile. Fry until golden brown and turn to brown the other side. Drain on several thicknesses of paper towels. Keep warm on a platter in a 250 degree oven. You may serve these with a sauce, but we love them just as is.

In Mexico, autumn's harvest of apples, pears, peaches, pomegranates and walnuts is celebrated by making chiles en nogada or chiles in walnut sauce. It is an exquisite, classic dish that will surprise anyone who has stereotyped views of Mexican cuisine, and will greatly please those who do not.

CHILES EN NOGADA

Prepare crema following the directions for homemade *crème fraîche* in recipe for Swiss Cream Enchiladas.

Walnut Sauce:

2 cups homemade crème fraîche,
     OR   an 8 ounce package of cream cheese
          softened and blended with 1 cup sour cream
1 1/2 cups walnuts, minced finely

Just before serving the chiles en nogada, you will need to stir the minced nuts into the crema or cream cheese mixture. Do not grind the nuts and crema together in a blender as the nuts will lose their character.

Preparing the Chiles:

12 medium - sized fresh green chiles, pasilla or poblano

Follow the directions given in Chapter IV for flaming or searing the chiles. Remove skins, seeds and veins. If you sear by the hot oil technique, be sure you blot off all excess oil. Set chiles aside in refrigerator. This step can be done a day ahead.

Preparing the Pork Picadillo Filling:

2 pounds boneless pork such as shoulder

1/2 onion stuck with 2 cloves

1 clove garlic

2 teaspoons salt

---

1 medium onion, minced

2 cloves garlic, minced

2 tablespoons oil

1 teaspoon cinnamon

1 teaspoon ground cloves

1 1/2 teaspoons salt

1 pound fresh tomatoes, peeled, seeded and chopped

freshly ground black pepper

1/2 cup raisins, plumped in 1/4 cup hot, dry sherry

1/2 cup blanched almonds, lightly toasted and chopped

1 fresh pear, chopped

1 fresh peach, chopped

1 ripe pomegranate, seeds removed for garnish

parsley sprigs for garnish

Cover meat, onion, garlic and salt with cold water and simmer for 1 1/2 hours or until tender. Cool in broth. Chop with sharp knife or in food processor. Do NOT use ground pork as a substitute for the minced pork.

Saute the onion and garlic over low heat until soft. Turn heat up, add the pork and saute until the meat is slightly browned. Add spices, raisins, almonds and tomatoes. Simmer for about 15 minutes or until juices are reduced. Remove from heat and stir in the minced fruit which must remain intact and not mushy.

You may cook the above picadillo in advance and keep it chilled in the refrigerator. But before assembling the entire dish you must wrap the chiles, which by now you have filled with the picadillo, in foil and heat them in a 350 degree oven for 15 minutes. Neither the chiles nor the picadillo should be used cold from the refrigerator.

Arrange the stuffed chiles on a serving platter. Stir the finely minced walnuts into the crema and pour the cool sauce over the chiles. Sprinkle the pomegranate seeds over the top and arrange the parsley around the edge of the platter.

As a young woman, I traveled to Mexico to study Spanish and lived in the colonial town of San Miguel de Allende. My brief stay of the intended three months lengthened into four years and I acquired an Irish husband. My early love of food blossomed in Mexico and I was so charmed by the heaps of vegetables and fruit in the open air markets, my baskets would be overflowing with chiles, eggplants, pineapples, mangoes of various hue and color and any other fruits which caught my eye.

The well-stocked ice box and larder led to experiments – with my new husband urging both me and Pueblito on to cooking extravaganzas. Some of our interpretations are more loyal than others to the originals.

Once you are no longer intimidated by the idea of breaking up dried chiles and blending them into a sauce, mole poblano will not seem such a faraway dish. Sometimes, the most troublesome aspect of mole is assembling all the ingredients and finding a good variety of chiles. I have often made a good mole, though sacreligious, using only pasilla chiles with a couple of mulatos. We love the elegant, classic mole poblano that is served in Mexico over the top of braised turkey, but we are quite fond of the peasant version served by our maid, Pueblito, who is now just a memory of our years spent in Mexico. She would simmer pieces of chicken for hours in a dark mole sauce until it heavily penetrated the meat becoming almost a stew.

Every Mexican, including your chile vendor in the marketplace, considers it his national duty to give you his unique version of mole, which might include bananas, peanuts, red tomatoes – or green tomatoes – several varieties of chiles and an endless list of secret ingredients to compete with ancient recipes involving as many as twenty-nine ingredients. When you put together your mole, resist the temptation to add too much of any one ingredient, especially chiles, or the delicate balance will be lost.

PEASANT MOLE

4 ancho chiles, dried

6 mulato chiles, dried

4 pasilla chiles, dried

Toast the chiles on a griddle or in a heavy cast iron pan. Keep turning so they soften, but do not burn. Rinse well to remove all dust and grit. Break each chile into two or three pieces, removing stems and seeds. Place in a large bowl and cover with boiling water. Soak for 1 - 2 hours. While they are soaking, prepare the rest of the ingredients.

4 cloves

1/2 cinnamon stick

6 tablespoons sesame seeds, toasted
> *(reserve 2 tablespoons for garnish)*

3 cloves garlic, toasted

4 medium, ripe tomatoes
> *(seared over gas flame - or roasted in broiler for 15*
> *minutes - peeled, seeded)*

1/2 cup almonds, toasted

2 tablespoons pine nuts, toasted lightly

1 stale tortilla, torn into pieces

1 slice of firm bread (such as French) torn into pieces

3 tablespoons raisins

1 1/2 ounces Mexican chocolate

3 - 5 cups homemade chicken or turkey broth

Using the same heavy pan you used for toasting the chiles, toast the seeds, nuts and bread. Or you can save time by putting them in little pans and toasting them in a 350 degree oven for about 10 minutes. Soak the raisins in hot water. Using a spice grinder, grind the cooled seeds, nuts and spices. If you do not have such a grinder, you may use a food processor although it will not pulverize the seeds to a powder. An electric coffee mill also works beautifully for this job. Grind the soaked chiles in four batches using a blender. Add 3/4 cup chicken or turkey broth to each batch to make a smooth puree. When you are pureeing the last batch of chiles, add all the ground seeds, nuts, spices, toasted garlic, tortilla pieces and bread pieces. Blend and then add the tomatoes and soaked raisins. Blend this mixture with the rest of the chile puree, adding more broth anytime it appears too thick. Blend in three batches.

Heat 2 tablespoons of oil in a heavy pot, add mole sauce and cook briskly for a few minutes, stirring constantly so it does not burn. Add the Mexican chocolate and more broth by the cupful, depending on how thick your sauce is and how much liquid you had to add during the pureeing process. It is best to only add a little broth at a time. Simmer the mole sauce for 1 hour, to strengthen the marriage of flavors. The added chocolate is an ancient trick, serving to calm the piquancy of the chiles. While the mole is simmering, prepare the chicken or turkey. You can make the mole sauce a day or two before you need it. It also freezes very well, and a bit of mole sauce is excellent stirred into an enchilada sauce or chile and beans.

Preparing the Turkey or Chicken for Mole

1 8 pound turkey OR 2 3 1/2 pound chickens
OR 4 whole chicken breasts OR 4 Cornish hens
1 onion
2 chipotle chiles, canned (see Shopping Sources)
chicken or turkey stock
4 to 6 quart cooking pot with lid

Reserve any gizzards, hearts, necks, backs and wings to make the stock, which you can make the day before you need it by simmering the above parts with a chopped carrot, onion, celery and bay leaf for a couple of hours.

If you are using a small turkey or two chickens, disjoint them into smaller pieces. Brown the pieces until golden in hot oil in your cooking pot. If you are using game hens or chicken breasts, they must also be browned. Drain off the oil and add 1 to 4 cups of stock, depending upon the amount of meat you are braising. The meat does not need to be covered with liquid. In braising, you only need a couple of inches of stock at the bottom of the pot so it will serve to steam the meat, not boil it. To the pot add the onion and the chipotle chiles and braise on very low heat for the following time periods: 20 minutes for chicken breasts, 30 - 35 minutes for game hens, 35 - 45 minutes for chicken parts, and 1 hour for turkey parts.

If I am preparing the chicken parts, I shorten the braising time to 25 minutes and then place the chicken in a pot with the mole to simmer for a couple of hours. The mole will become

even more enriched and the chicken will stay juicy and delight-
fully imbued with the myriad of mole flavors. Add more broth
to the pot if the sauce appears too thick.

If you want to serve your mole in the classic style rather
than the above peasant version, simply finish braising your fowl
in the pot then place it on a serving platter and mask it
generously with the mole sauce. Before serving, whatever
style, sprinkle the mole with the reserved, toasted sesame seeds
and garnish with something green. Mole is delicious with plain
rice or tamales.

Once, in one of my favorite restaurants in Mexico City -
Las Cazuelas - I watched two very stout men, obviously brothers, savor huge bowls of green mole. They only disturbed their
intense concentration to call for second and third helpings and
more tortillas, which were being handpatted in the kitchen.
Each brother, in turn, would unfold the cloth of the basket to
remove a warm tortilla. It was then torn in half, then in
quarters and in a marvelous twist of thumb and forefinger, a
scoop for mole was formed in one rolling motion. In one
sensuous bite, the scoop was gone; on to the next scoop and,
thusly, baskets and baskets of tortillas went to their fate.

Green mole is called green because the tomatillos are so important to the dish. It is much simpler to prepare than classic mole and the sauce is wonderful over many things, including steamed cauliflower.

GREEN MOLE

1 pork loin, approximately 3 pounds
oil
1 onion stuck with 2 cloves
1 clove garlic
1 teaspoon salt

Cut pork into two-inch cubes and dry well with paper towels. Brown lightly in oil. Drain off any excess oil and add 1 1/2 cups cold water along with the onion, cloves, garlic and salt. Simmer on low heat for 1 1/2 hours or until the meat is tender. Test by poking with fork.

Sauce

1/2 cup raw pine nuts, finely ground
1/2 cup blanched almonds, finely ground
2 cups cooked tomatillos
   (simmer 2 pounds of fresh tomatillos in 2 inches of boiling water 10 minutes - don't overcook or they will disintegrate)
   OR use 2 large cans tomatillos
2 cloves garlic

1 medium onion

1/2 teaspoon comino seeds

2 - 3 fresh serrano chiles

   OR use canned jalapeno chiles

1 teaspoon salt

2 cups chicken broth

1/4 cup cilantro, minced

Toast the pine nuts by stirring in a heavy skillet over medium heat. Remove and set aside. Toast the almonds until they are golden. Grind the cooled seeds and nuts in a food processor or spice grinder until of fine texture. Place the cooked tomatillos, onion, garlic, chiles, comino in a blender and puree. In large pot, add the puree, the ground nuts and seeds, to 1 cup of chicken broth. Add the cooked cubes of pork and simmer for 20 minutes, adding more broth to thin out the sauce if necessary. Stir in the minced cilantro during the last 5 minutes of cooking. Serve with Mexican or Spanish-style rice and a basket of warm tortillas.

As long as you have tortillas around, you will end up with a few stale ones and nothing should go to waste. In Mexico, stale tortillas are cut up and fried into chips or tostaditas; they are ground up in sauces, or lightly fried and used as a garnish for soups or to make our very favorite for leftover tortillas, chilaquiles. In this recipe, a sauce very similar to that of green mole is created. You can play with chilaquiles, adding herbs, spices and chiles to your own taste. For a brunch dish to accompany Bloody Marys, chilaquiles are perfect.

CHILAQUILES

12 stale or day-old tortillas

1 cup vegetable oil

1 medium onion, chopped + 1 clove garlic, minced

1 10 ounce can tomatillos

3 jalapeno chiles, canned

      OR   2 - 3 fresh jalapeno or serrano chiles

1 cup sour cream

3/4 cup hot chicken broth, canned or homemade

4 sprigs fresh cilantro, chopped

1 sprig fresh epazote (optional)

2/3 cup sharp cheese (Cheddar, Fontina, or Greek Kasseri)

Stacking up four tortillas at a time, cut into strips or triangles. Fry in 1 inch of hot oil until the strips are firm, but not browned. Drain on paper towels. Repeat until all tortilla strips are fried, adding more oil if necessary. Drain the tomatillos and roughly puree in a blender with the herbs, chiles and garlic. Saute the tomatillo mixture in 1 tablespoon of hot oil for a few minutes, adding 1/4 cup of the chicken broth. In a large, deep skillet or enameled iron pan, layer first some of the fried tortilla strips, part of the tomatillo mixture, cheese, sour cream, chopped onion, the rest of the tortilla strips, ending with the rest of the sauce and cheese. Add the remaining chicken broth and simmer the chilaquiles until they have absorbed the juices and softened. You may also bake them in a 350 degree oven for about 20 minutes. Do not cook chilaquiles too long or keep in a warming oven as they will dry out. In

Mexico, the dish might be garnished with sprigs of cilantro, quartered hard-boiled eggs or radishes.

Note: To create a meal of more substance, add pieces of leftover, poached chicken.

Epazote is the unusual herb used frequently in Mexican cooking, particularly in Yucatan so those of us who have admired epazote have had to seek out the herb and its seeds, available at Taylor's Herb Farm in California.   There is no substitute for epazote, no other herb of comparable flavor. My vegetable man, who is from Merida, Yucatan, brought me a small plant from his garden in Oxnard and I now have about thirty plants thriving in my yard - a jungle of epazote which grows like a weed. Running out of recipes to use it for, I was quite happy when a friend told me of her idea for burritos.

ELEGANT MUSHROOM CHILE BURRITOS

1 pound fresh mushrooms, cleaned and sliced
1 clove garlic, minced
3 green onions with green tops, sliced
2 Ortega green chiles, seeded and chopped

4 tablespoons butter

dash Worcestershire sauce

1/2 lemon

1/4 cup dry sherry

salt

freshly ground black pepper

2 tablespoons fresh epazote, chopped

1/2 cup sour cream

6 flour tortillas

> *(warmed by wrapping in foil and heating in oven for 15 minutes at 350 degrees)*

Saute mushrooms, epazote leaves, scallions, garlic and seasonings. Squeeze lemon juice over all. Saute 3 minutes. Add the 1/4 cup sherry and allow it to reduce. Remove from heat. If there is more than a tablespoon of liquid in the pan, drain off a little. Add 1/2 cup sour cream and mix, putting it back on the heat for just a minute (the sour cream will thin out if overheated). Fill and roll each tortilla as for burritos.

Grandpa, in his younger days.

CHAPTER V

THE FOOD OF FESTIVITIES

Feasts, Birthdays and Weddings

ne of our family weddings, more than a century ago, became a family legend that shaped history for all of us. It was during one of his lengthy morning breakfasts that Grandpa told me about the wedding of María Higuera, my great-grandmother.

Grandpa cut a cube of cheese, impaled it onto the sharp, pronged fork that was the only utensil used for this ritual, and held the cheese in his cup of hot coffee. After savoring the warm cheese, he offered, "If it was not for María Higuera's wedding, we would still have leagues of land. But she was the pet of ten children and Don Valentín gave her a royal wedding."

From the time a Spanish girl in California could ride a horse, she was told of her wedding day when she would ride to the cathedral amidst frolicking horsemen. Promised were new combs of tortoise shell and pearl for her hair; a dress, not of white, but bright and sunny colors. To make her mysterious, she would be given a silk shawl from China.

There sat Grandpa, in his pressed trousers and blue cambric shirt, detailing his mother's wedding as if he had been there, so many times had she told him the story during sleepless nights in the old adobe.

María's beauty was part of the legend although nothing remains to attest to this as all the treasured tintypes were destroyed when the one hundred year old ranch house burned in the 1930's. In the only surviving photograph of María, taken when she was in her sixties, she stands proud and handsome, wearing a black silk dress like those worn by dueñas. I have held this photograph, trying to discern her spirit and the legend haunting her.

No one can agree on the number of days of feasting and dancing that followed María's marriage to Nicolas Chavarria, a Chilean, in the spring of 1865. The days were many. Six women were kept busy cooking for a week, preparing all of the traditional foods – the red enchiladas, empanadas in honor of Nicolas, corn tamales of various flavors, hundreds of flour tortillas; meats rubbed with herbs, cakes and imported sweets brought from San Francisco, and on the wedding day itself, a bull's head barbequed in a pit. There were various wines,

131

especially the favorite sweet wine resembling Malaga, and angélica to accompany the cakes and fruits.

The different types of foods were offered in miniature shelters constructed of tules and grasses with colorful ribbons hung in the doorways beckoning the tasters inside. The wine hut operated on the unwritten law that if anyone should overindulge or get unbecomingly drunk, they would have to leave the feasting until they could act respectably again.

On this special day for María, Don Valentín allowed her to choose the honored gentleman who would ride with her to the mission church. She picked Uncle Joe. She was helped onto her own petite saddle, but when she placed her slipper into the loop of pink ribbon used as the stirrup, the ribbon broke. She said later it was an omen of bad luck. But Uncle Joe mounted his favorite and most beautiful horse and sitting protectively at María's back, rode with her to the Mission Santa Clara, three leagues away.

The bridegroom Nicolas, María's brothers, her cousins and playful friends accompanied them, galloping on in front, turning around to gallop right up to Maria and Uncle Joe, bringing their horses to a dead stop with a touch of the hand. This was no solemn wedding procession.

After the wedding ceremony, María and Nicolas mounted their own favorite horses, festooned with ribbons and waiting outside the mission doors. They were surrounded at once by their attendants with the rest of the wedding party following.

Some people waited for them along the road, holding up arches of flowers for them to pass under. Many of the older ladies rode in wagons and carriages down the dusty roads. It took three and a half hours to get from Mission Santa Clara to the ranch in a wagon, a considerable journey which was made by the family every Sunday for Mass. By horseback it took only a couple of hours.

When María and Nicolas finally arrived at Rancho Los Tularcitos, the celebration which was to go on for a week began. They were not given any romantic seclusion for days. There was to be only eating, drinking, dancing, picnicking, bullfighting and more dancing.

The rancheros and Californios were given to dancing for many nights at a time, until the men dropped. There is no mention of the women dropping, only that they wore out a succession of silk dancing slippers.

For the celebration, a wooden dance floor was laid out in a sheltered spot, hung all around with ribbons, silks and boughs. The best musicians were brought out to play for the bridal couple. As night came, torches made of long poles with knots of pitch-pine fastened to the tops, were flamed and the burning resin of the torches mingled with the scent of flowers. They danced until daybreak with everyone taking a few hours of sleep until the mid-morning picnic in the foothills, attended on horseback. The dueñas were finally snoozing on the verandah.

In the afternoon of the second day, there was a bullfight

133

staged in the special arena, a shallow pit surrounded by an adobe wall, south of the ranch house.

As evening brought darkness, the dancing began again and continued through the night. And according to legend, Don Valentín spent all of his remaining gold doubloons for the entertainment and feeding of his weeklong guests. Vaqueros were sent to town for more wine, brandy, cakes, cigars or anything a lady might wish such as a new pair of dancing shoes. Tabs were signed and mysterious contracts with quadrupling interests were agreed to against the land.

I had listened to this tale for years . . . . María Higuera's wedding had brought ruin to the family. I began to question and get angry for María and the legend she carried.

My brother's wife, Stephanie, spent hundreds of hours in geneological research and compilation of family history. It became more and more evident that ruin did not come from a lavish wedding, but from a multitude of enemies. Don Valentín had a taste for gambling. Or perhaps it was the high taxes and the land-hungry swindlers. Or the proud house bursting with children. Or the infringement of a civilization not given to dancing for days, but when Don Valentín turned around his land was gone and so was the nineteenth century.

For over one hundred years, the wedding myth was repeated, even accepted by María and Nicolas who continued to live on the remaining land of the ranch. But there was always reason to celebrate someone's birthday, the feast day of a saint, the honor of a distinguished visitor, but never again was there such a wedding to equal María Higuera's.

The highlight of all celebrations was food – elaborate food which took more time to prepare, was more unusual, and often called for ingredients which had to be sent for from San Francisco.

Nicolas always insisted on celebrating the National Day of Chile, his homeland, on September 18th. A traditional dish, pastel de choclo or chileño pie was served amidst shouts of "Viva Chile." The pie was prepared in huge amounts and the Chilean flag was given a place of honor where all of the guests and family could view it while eating the chileña pie. A Chilean diplomat visiting from San Francisco was served the pie during one of the festive barbeques and he was quoted as saying he became so homesick while eating pastel de choclo, it brought tears to his eyes. This could be partly legend and partly the great emotion shown by Latins for their food.

GREAT–GRANDMA SILVA'S CHILEÑA PIE

This hearty dish is basically a meat pie using ground fresh corn in place of pastry so the corn topping forms a thin golden layer over the filling. As you bite into the pie, you will discover three different layers – one of sweet, delicate corn, juicy chicken, and a bottom layer of spicy picadillo.

2 1/2 - 3 pounds round steak, thickly cut

1 onion, chopped

1 clove garlic

1 carrot, chopped

cold water

---

1 onion, chopped finely

1 clove garlic, minced

2 teaspoons oregano

2 teaspoons comino, mashed in mortar

2 tablespoons pure chile powder (NOT blend)

1 teaspoon salt

1/4 cup raisins, plumped in hot water

Cover the meat with cold water, onion, garlic and carrot and simmer for 1 and 1/2 hours on the lowest heat. Cool in the broth. Remove the meat, reserving broth. Chop meat finely using a chef's knife. The meat will shred better if you chop it while it is still warm. Saute the chopped onion and minced garlic in olive oil until softened. Add the herbs and spices, the chile powder, salt and the minced meat. Briefly cook together to blend the flavors. Remove from the heat and add 1/2 cup broth and the raisins. If the meat mixture appears dry, add more broth. Grandmama always said the meat should glisten or it was not moist enough. Set aside and prepare the chicken. It is helpful if you prepare the picadillo and the chicken the day before you will be assembling the pie.

3 pounds chicken, disjointed

3 cups chicken stock or water

2 tablespoons olive oil

1 fresh jalapeño, minced and seeds removed

salt and pepper

Cut breast into four parts and place with all the chicken pieces into a large pot covering with cold water. Poach for 25 minutes and cool in the broth. Remove chicken from the bones and saute in the olive oil along with the minced pepper. Season with salt and pepper. Set aside while you prepare the corn.

10 ears fresh corn

2 tablespoons butter

salt (approximately 1 teaspoon)

1 tablespoon sugar

1/2 cup thick cream

1 tablespoon fresh basil, snipped

     OR   1 teaspoon dry basil

1 tablespoon brown sugar

Grate the corn on a special corn grater or use a small knife (see directions given in Green Corn Tamale recipe). Melt butter in nonstick pan and add the corn and its liquid. Add the cream, the salt and sugar. Saute the corn - cream mixture until excess liquid has evaporated and the corn is thickened. Stir in the basil.

Grease a 10 x 14 inch baking dish and spread the picadillo over the bottom. Next, layer the chicken and pepper over the beef picadillo. Lastly, spread the corn – cream mixture in a thin layer over the top. Sprinkle with brown sugar. Sometimes Grandmama would spread slivers of sweet basil into the corn. Bake the pie at 375 degrees for approximately 30 minutes or until the corn layer is golden brown and crusty on top.

In bygone days, tamales were not ordinary fare, but food reserved for holidays. There was never a Christmas or New Year's celebration without them. The making of tamales was never considered a job because it meant a roomful of laughing people, all assembled at the big kitchen table which was spread with newspapers, damp corn husks and rolls of string. Everyone had his own task – spreading dough on the husks, putting on the filling, rolling of the husks, or tying the tamale with string. And there was lots of yelling out of advice as to just how the task could best be accomplished, with the passing of the port wine giving added bravado to all the comments. The person who added meat filling was scrutinized the most because if there wasn't enough filling everyone complained, and if there was too much it leaked out all over the tamale pot.

Our family always spread extra dough on additional corn husks and tied these around the tamale to make it extra large. This practice also safeguarded against chile juices leaking into the pot. These California-style tamales were huge and I loved peeling off each leaf and eating that first pure corn essence with the little brown flecks.

The tamales were steamed for about an hour while Grandmama raved about too many people coming to check the pot. Eventually she gave away little morsels from the tamales she opened on the kitchen counter to check for doneness.

BEEF TAMALES

3 1/2 pounds chuck, clod, seven-bone roast or flank steak
2 tablespoons oil
1 onion
1 clove garlic
oregano
freshly ground pepper

Cut meat into 4-inch pieces. Dry well. Brown in batches in hot oil, setting aside. When browning is complete combine meat with rest of ingredients in a large pot and cover with cold water or beef stock, if you have it. Simmer slowly for 1 1/2 to 2 hours. Cool in broth. Reserve broth.

For chile sauce:

15 pasilla chiles (or you may use California chiles)

1 cup reserved beef broth

2 tablespoons flour

2 tablespoons oil

1 clove garlic mashed with 1 teaspoon salt

2 teaspoons oregano

1 teaspoon comino seeds, toasted

1 large can black olives

Make chile puree following directions in recipe for Red Chile Puree, the Rancho Staple (Chapter IV). Reserve 1/4 cup of chile puree to add to the tamale dough later. Brown flour lightly in hot oil. Cook roux for a couple of minutes then add garlic, oregano, comino and chile puree. Simmer for 20 minutes. Using two sharp forks, break up the cubes of beef and place in the chile sauce. If sauce is too thick dilute with a little beef broth. Simmer for 1/2 hour more and set aside to cool before making your tamale dough. I usually do this step the day before making tamales.

For tamale dough:

Large package of cornhusks
    (buy the widest and longest husks available)

1 1/2 pounds lard

4 pounds fresh masa

1 cup reserved beef broth

1/4 cup reserved chile puree

2 tablespoons salt

6 ice cubes, crushed

Soak husks in warm water for 45 minutes to 1 hour or until quite pliable. Set aside after draining well. Beat lard for 5 minutes with electric mixer until light and fluffy. Dissolve salt in broth. Add masa slowly to the whipped lard, beating with mixer (heavy duty mixer is best) for about 5 more minutes. (In the dark past, this beating was done by a couple of women taking turns, using a large wooden spoon.) Pour in the salted broth and the crushed ice, whipping again for 2 - 3 minutes. To test for lightness of the batter, drop a teaspoonful into a glass of cold water. It has been sufficiently whipped if the dough floats on top. Then stir in the chile puree to give your tamales a rosy hue.

Assembling tamales:

Drained cornhusks

Kitchen string

Steamer kettle with basket

Lay out the damp husks on a flat surface, choosing the largest husks or overlapping two. Patch up any holes with a strip off a husk and a bit of masa dough. Spread out about 3 tablespoons masa dough, leaving a 1 inch border on one side. Do not spread to the edge of both sides of the husk or the dough will squeeze out when rolled and tied. After placing a spoonful of filling in the center, roll up and tie both ends. If you love the steamed masa as I do, spread extra dough on another husk and wrap it around the already filled tamale and then tie. Grandmama's double-layered tamales were a dinner in themselves.

Line the bottom of the steamer basket (you have already placed 3 inches of hot water and a penny in the pot) and the sides of the pot with damp husks. Put the tamales in loosely, standing them on end and cover with more husks. Steam for 1 hour and 15 minutes covered tightly. Listen to the talking of the pot to make sure the boiling water does not evaporate. Keep some hot water in your tea kettle in case of need. To test for doneness, open a steamed tamale and let it rest a few minutes. If the dough holds together and pulls away from the husk, it is done. A cooked tamale should not seem sticky.

The tamale is the most tender and delicate when it comes fresh from the steaming kettle and no one should miss having one at that moment so eat immediately to properly enjoy the freshness. But if you must, you may keep them in the refrigerator for a couple of days and reheat in a steamer or in the oven wrapped in foil. Tamales freeze well. To heat frozen tamales, wrap in foil and heat in 350 degree oven for 1/2 hour. If your leftover tamales seem dry, layer them in a casserole with some diced green chiles, sauteed onion, sour cream and Teleme cheese.

Miniature sweet tamales were made for feast days, saint's days, and as happy food for a party. They could be nibbled on with a glass of wine throughout an evening of celebration.

I made the wonderful discovery of how good they were mixed with crumbled, day-old cornbread, raisins, pine nuts, spices and stuffed into a holiday turkey.

SWEET TAMALES

Filling:

1/2 cup white Sultana raisins
1/2 cup dark raisins
1/4 cup sherry

Dough:

3 cups masa harina blended with
2 1/2 cups warm water
6 ounces (1 1/2 stick) unsalted butter, room temperature
2/3 cup brown sugar
1/2 teaspoon salt
dash of cinnamon powder
1/4 cup blanched almonds, ground
2 crushed ice cubes
(mash in a towel with a heavy mallet)
2 - 4 tablespoons milk
1/2 teaspoon baking powder

1/2 package dried cornhusks

soaked for 1 hour in warm water

Soak raisins in hot sherry until plumped. Using electric mixer, whip the butter until light and fluffy. Add the sugar and salt then the masa in small amounts while you continue to whip the mixture for 8 - 10 minutes. Add the ground almonds. Add the milk to the masa mixture along with the crushed ice. Stir in the baking powder. To test for dough lightness, drop a spoonful of dough into a glass of cold water. If the dough floats to the top, it is ready.

Drain the soaked cornhusks on paper towels. You will need fewer cornhusks because sweet tamales are meant to be eaten as appetizers or for a light dessert, not a whole meal.

Spread 2 tablespoons of dough on each husk. Dough should be about 1/8 inch thick, but not run to the edge of the husk. If a husk is too narrow, overlap it with another husk. Add 1 teaspoon raisins and pecans (optional) to the center of the dough and fold over the edges of the husk. Tie up the ends with kitchen string.

Place several damp husks on the bottom of a steamer basket. Stack the tamales on end. Cover with more soaked husks and an old tea towel. Steam for about 1 hour at a low simmer. Makes 18 - 20 small, sweet tamales.

STUFFING (RELLENO) FOR HOLIDAY TURKEY

8 leftover sweet tamales

3 cups leftover, day-old cornbread

1 teaspoon comino seeds, crushed in mortar

1 tablespoon chile powder

1 medium onion, chopped

2 tablespoons butter or oil

1/4 cup black raisins

1/4 cup pine nuts, lightly toasted
      (or you may use chopped pecans)

1 egg

1/4 cup warm chicken broth

Saute onion in butter until very soft. Add the chile powder, the comino seeds, the raisins and pine nuts and saute with the onions for a few more minutes. In a large bowl, stir together the crumbled tamales, cornbread, sauteed onions, nuts, raisins, egg and broth. Add more broth or milk if the mixture seems dry. Taste for seasoning, making it as spicy as you like. Add more raisins or nuts if your taste dictates, or some highly seasoned pork sausage which you have fried and drained. This is enough stuffing for a 12 pound bird.

TRADITIONAL CORNBREAD

1 cup sifted flour, all-purpose

1 cup stoneground cornmeal

1 tablespoon sugar

4 teaspoons baking powder

1 teaspoon salt

2 eggs, beaten

1 cup milk

1/4 cup oil or melted butter

Sift dry ingredients together. Combine liquid ingredients and pour all at once onto the flour mixture, stirring lightly just to blend. Pour into a greased 8 inch square pan and bake at 425 degrees for about 20 - 25 minutes. If you are using for cornbread stuffing, wait until the cornbread is cooled and then cut out what is approximately 3 cups of bread. Break it up on a cookie sheet so that it will dry. You may have to put it in a 300 degree oven for about 25 minutes to dry more thoroughly before using it in the stuffing.

The following recipe is from Grandmama's mother, Cecilia, who came to California as an eight year old child on a ship from Valparaiso, Chile. One of the few things she remembered of her homeland were empanadas. The pastry is light but sturdy enough to hold lots of filling. They were made by the dozens around the holidays or to carry on picnics. Grandmama's always held almost a half cup of meat picadillo and so were justly loved by all the men. Grandmama would have nothing to do with making empanaditas with their tablespoon of filling. Of all her recipes, this is one of my favorites.

GREAT-GRANDMA SILVA'S EMPANADAS

Picadillo filling:

2 1/2 pounds round steak

1 clove garlic

1 onion stuck with 3 cloves

1 onion, minced

1 carrot, chopped

3 tablespoons olive oil

2 - 3 teaspoons oregano

2 - 3 teaspoons comino seeds, crushed in mortar

1 - 2 tablespoons ground chile powder

1 teaspoon salt

1/2 cup sherry

1 cup black raisins

2 tablespoons sugar

1/4 cup slivered almonds

1 cup sliced black olives

    OR   1/2 cup sliced stuffed green olives

    (Grandmama's favorite)

Empanada dough:

3 cups flour

1/4 cup shortening

2 tablespoons butter

About 1/2 cup + 1 tablespoon water

    blended with 1 teaspoon salt

For the picadillo filling, place the round steak which you have cut into six pieces, in a large pot and cover with cold water. Add the whole onion, garlic and carrot. Simmer gently for 2 hours. Cool in the broth. Drain off the broth and reserve. Using a large, sharp knife chop the meat very finely. Because of the long, slow cooking, this should not be a difficult process. Grandmama minced her meat in a small wooden bowl using a hand chopper. Chop the meat while it is still warm.

Saute the minced onion until soft with the herbs and seeds in olive oil then add the chopped meat and chile powder. Cook together about 15 minutes, adding enough of the reserved meat broth to make the mixture glisten, but it should not be soggy. While the picadillo is cooking, steep the raisins in hot sherry and after they are plumped, add them to the meat. Remove the picadillo from the heat and stir in the almonds and chopped olives. Add the salt and sugar and then taste the picadillo for correct seasoning. Add more spices or chile powder if you like. If the picadillo seems dry, moisten with a little of the raisin sherry or the meat broth; however, if the picadillo is too soggy the juices will leak through the crust of the empanadas. This filling can be made a day ahead.

For the empanada dough, rub the fat into the flour until crumbly. Gradually add enough salted water to make a soft, pliable dough. Knead on a floured board for about 1 minute or until the dough is smooth.

Break off a piece of dough and roll into a 6 inch circle. Place 1/2 cup of filling on half of the circle. Fold over the top half, pinching over the edges, pressing to seal with a fork.

Fry in deep fat or oil which you have heated to almost the smoking point. Fry each empanada for 2 - 3 minutes, spooning the hot oil over the surface and then turning. Cook until golden. Remove and drain on paper towels, blotting off the surface of the empanada with more paper towels. Sprinkle lightly with sugar. You can serve them immediately or cool and store in the refrigerator. Reheat on a baking sheet in a 350 degree oven for 10 minutes. Makes about 12 very large empanadas.

We looked forward to the peak of autumn as we watched the orange balls in the field grow and grow. Pumpkin pies occasionally graced Mama's table, but for Grandmama there were only warm, spicy pumpkin empanadas, dusted with cinnamon, leaving us to decide whether we liked the meat and raisin empanadas best or these sweet confections. We never decided.

Grandmama's little pies contained wild, sweet anise as did many other Spanish - California desserts, because this herb grew wild in the hills and valleys and was there for the picking. As with good cinnamon, anise possesses its own natural sweetness.

PUMPKIN EMPANADAS

Filling:

16 ounces of canned pumpkin puree
    OR   2 cups of mashed, steamed, fresh pumpkin
3/4 cup brown sugar
2 teaspoons of chopped, feathery leaves of wild anise
    OR   1/2 teaspoon cinnamon
1/4 teaspoon nutmeg, freshly grated
1 egg
1 1/2 teaspoons pure vanilla

Pastry:

2 cups flour
2 tablespoons sugar
2 teaspoons baking powder
1/2 teaspoon salt
1/2 cup shortening
1/4 cup butter, cut into small pieces
1 tablespoon brandy mixed with 3 tablespoons milk
1 egg, beaten with 1 tablespoon water
2 tablespoons sugar mixed with 1 teaspoon cinnamon

If you are using fresh pumpkin, cut it into 2-inch pieces from which you have removed all fibers and seeds. Steam over boiling water until tender (about 35 minutes). Remove rind from cooked pumpkin after it has cooled. Puree in a food processor or blender. Blend all filling ingredients together and simmer in a saucepan for 3 minutes over medium heat stirring constantly. Cool before making turnovers.

Preheat oven to 450 degrees. Sift dry ingredients together. Cut shortening and butter into flour mixture using a pastry blender or two knives. The mixture should resemble coarse meal. Add the brandy-milk mixture a little at a time, stirring briskly to distribute the moisture. You want the dough to just be held together. Do not overblend. Place dough on floured board and knead 3 or 4 times, using the heel of your hand. Chill for 30 minutes.

Roll out thinly on floured board. Cut into 4 - 5 inch circles. Place about 2 tablespoons of pumpkin filling on 1/2 of the circle. Fold over. Rub edge with egg wash and press with a fork to seal the edges. Brush with more egg wash and place on a heavy baking sheet. Bake for 15 - 18 minutes or until golden. Sprinkle with cinnamon - sugar. Serve warm. Makes 14 - 16 small empanadas.

When I left home and went to Mexico, I tried to duplicate Grandmama's rice. It wasn't the same and even though it was said to be good by everyone who tasted it, I was sadly disappointed. Then one day while I was working at the dining room table, a wonderful toasty rice smell drifted in from the kitchen where our new maid, Maria, was preparing rice for comida. I rushed to the kitchen and found Maria frying the rice in a heavy Mexican cazuela, a pottery vessel. All of a sudden, the secret to Grandmama's rice - something I had overlooked - was given to me. The rice must be fried in oil until golden before it is simmered in liquid. Only then will it have that certain flavor as if some unusual, mysterious spice has been added.

GRANDMAMA'S SPANISH RICE

1 cup long-grain white rice
(Louisiana rice is very delectable)
1/4 cup olive oil
1 clove garlic mashed with 1 1/2 teaspoon salt
1/2 onion, minced
3 teaspoons ground chile powder
2 1/2 cups water

Fry the rice in hot olive oil until it is golden and there is a whiff of a popcorn smell. Add the onion, garlic and salt and saute a bit more. Then tip the pan and spoon off any excess oil. Add the chile powder and, according to Grandmama, "two fingers of water" which amounts to about 2 1/2 cups. Use stock if you have it. Allow the rice to cook on medium heat for 10 minutes or until you see little holes forming in the center, the sign the rice has absorbed most of the liquid. Turn the heat to low, put on a lid and steam for 10 minutes more. Turn off the heat, but leave the pot undisturbed for at least 20 minutes. No peeking. This extra time will allow the rice grains to steam and swell to lovely fluffiness.

This method for preparing Grandmama's rice is really necessary to arroz con pollo, our great family party dish.

Arroz con pollo was the favorite to serve to a large party in the evening when nothing could be barbequed outdoors on the parilla or grills. If you want to double the recipe, use a long roasting pan so the rice is not too deep and it will cook much fluffier. It is a delicious way to prepare rice – kind of a poor man's paella. The chicken is skinned so the flavors penetrate the meat more thoroughly, and rubbed with a seasoning paste; I have played with this recipe a lot, sometimes adding sauteed, sliced Italian sausage or spicy chorizo to the rice while it is steaming.

ARROZ CON POLLO

2 cloves garlic

1 teaspoon salt

2 teaspoons chile powder or 1 teaspoon creole powder

1/2 teaspoon comino seeds

1 tablespoon olive oil for sauteing

1 chicken (about 3 pounds) disjointed

2 tablespoons olive oil

1 small onion, minced

1 slice ham, cut into strips

2 Italian sweet sausages, sauteed, drained and sliced

> *OR 1/2 pound chorizo sausage, sauteed and drained*

1 cup long-grain rice

3 cups liquid (water or chicken stock)

2 tablespoons dry sherry

Mash garlic, salt, comino seeds, olive oil and chile powder or creole powder into a paste. (Creole powder is a blend of spices - paprika, cayenne pepper, thyme, onion powder and garlic powder - and is available in specialty food shops.) Rub this over all the chicken parts from which you have removed the skin. Allow to set at room temperature for 1/2 hour while flavors penetrate. Fry in olive oil until lightly browned. Remove and saute the onion and rice for 5 minutes over medium heat. Remove any excess oil. Return chicken to pan along with stock, sherry, ham and optional sausages. Bring to simmer on top of stove, cooking for 10 minutes. Cover tightly with lid or foil. Bake in a moderately hot oven - 350 degrees - for 45 minutes. Remove from oven and allow to rest covered for 10 minutes.

If there was to be a small celebration like a birthday party, with only a chosen few invited, Mama would do up a glorious paella. This was not ranch food. The dish is of Spanish origin and we jokingly called it a rich man's arroz con pollo.

You begin with the basic rice and chicken base and then add or subtract seafood as your pocketbook allows.

PAELLA

1 pound uncooked, medium shrimp

2 1/2 pounds chicken pieces

2 teaspoons oregano

2 cloves garlic

1/2 teaspoon freshly ground pepper

1 1/2 teaspoons salt

1 teaspoon vinegar

2 tablespoons olive oil

1/2 pound chorizo (see recipe index)

4 ounces sliced ham, cut into strips

1 dozen clams or mussels

1 pound scallops

4 - 6 lobster tails

3 medium tomatoes, peeled, seeded, chopped

OR use canned, plum tomatoes

1 onion, minced

1 stalk celery, chopped

1 bell pepper, chopped

2 1/2 cups long-grain rice

2 tablespoons capers

1 jar Spanish pimientos

1/2 teaspoon coriander

1/2 teaspoon salt

1/2 teaspoon saffron steeped in 1/4 cup hot water

5 1/2 - 6 cups boiling stock or water

1 bay leaf

1 cup of very small, frozen peas (defrosted)

Leave shrimp in shells. Pound the garlic, oregano, salt, pepper, vinegar and olive oil in mortar or grind in a food processor. Rub this paste over the well-dried chicken pieces. Heat 2 tablespoons olive oil in a large, heavy skillet or paella pan and brown the chicken.

In a separate skillet, fry the chorizo sausage. Drain on paper towels.

Scrub the clams.

Heat 1/4 cup olive oil in the paella pan (paellero) and saute the onion, celery and bell pepper until softened. Push vegetables aside. Add the rice and fry until golden brown (very important). Add the chopped tomatoes and cook for about 5 minutes. Next add the capers, coriander, salt, ham, the drained chorizo and 5 1/2 cups boiling water. At times, for part of the boiling water, I've substituted chicken broth, clam broth and left over stock from the boiling of the lobster tails. If you plan to use fresh scallops in your paella, poach them first in clam juice (bottled is fine) for 3 minutes and then use this poaching liquid for part of the liquid to cook your rice. Add the bay leaf and the saffron water. Place the chicken pieces on top of the rice, saving the seafood for the last.

156

Simmer the paella on low heat for 15 minutes then place in a preheated (350 degree) oven, covered with foil for another 10 - 15 minutes or until the rice is tender and fluffy. During the last 10 minutes, add the clams, shrimp, strips of pimiento, and the tiny peas. Cover with foil and return to the oven for 10 minutes. If you are fortunate enough to have lobster tails for your paella, cook them separately in boiling water to cover for 10 - 14 minutes. Place decorously on top of the paella just before serving. Do not throw away the lobster water. You may cook or reduce it down to half its amount and freeze it. Use for cooking rice, soups or chowders - or even your next paella. Remove paella from oven but do not remove foil for at least five minutes. Serve to 8 - 10 paella lovers.

Should you be in the mood for something out of the ordinary for your pork loin, the following will most definitely fill the bill. Roasted whole, rubbed with a seasoning paste, and baked in sealed clay as is done in Yucatan, will bring cheers from those gathered 'round your table. As you hammer away at your pork roast, your guests will be astounded and your children delighted. The roast will remain moist and flavored deliciously with the seasonings.

PORK ROAST YUCATAN STYLE

1 pork roast (3 - 4 pounds of loin)

2 tablespoons achiote paste

> *(known as adobo and available in some Mexican markets; if you can't find adobo, an alternate would be Hungarian paprika)*

1 1/2 tablespoons salt

3 tablespoons orange juice

1 tablespoon lemon or lime juice

1 tablespoon vinegar

1 tablespoon oregano

1 teaspoon allspice

1 teaspoon freshly ground black pepper

1 teaspoon ground cumin or crushed comino seeds

1 tablespoon garlic, minced

banana leaves or aluminum foil

Preheat your oven to 450 degrees. Using food processor or mortar, grind all the seasoning ingredients into a paste. Dry the roast well with paper towels and rub seasoning paste over the entire surface which you have pricked with a fork. Set aside while you prepare the clay.

If you are unable to find the achiote or adobo paste, your roast will not be an authentic Yucatan dish, but the Hungarian paprika makes a delicious alternative.

Baker's Clay:

3 1/2 cups all-purpose flour

1 1/2 cups salt

1 tablespoon comino seeds
   ground to powder (or ground cumin)

1 1/4 - 1 1/2 cups water

Combine dry ingredients. Add liquid in small amounts until dough holds together and can be gathered into a ball. Wrap in plastic wrap.

Assembly:

Wrap the pork roast in aluminum foil or blanched banana leaves. If you are using banana leaves, place them one at a time in a large pot of hot water only long enough to make them soft and pliable. Roll out clay dough on large piece of floured waxed paper until it measures about 20 x 18 inches. Arrange pork roast in center of dough. Fold dough up over the roast. Seal seams. Place, seam on bottom, in roasting pan that has been lined with more foil. Roast for 2 1/2 hours in a preheated 450 degree oven.

Remove pan from the oven and crack the clay in several places using a hammer. Peel off the foil or leaves. Allow roast to rest for at least 10 minutes before carving. Serve with tortillas, beans and salad. The seasoning deeply penetrates the meat which remains very moist.

If I had to pick a standout of all the faraway memories of Rancho Los Tularcitos, there would have to be near the top of the list a New Year's Eve with the flicker of kerosene lamps lighting up the long table graced by platters of palillis. puffy concoctions light enough to float into your mouth. We would poke our fingers into them and smash them in powdered sugar. Palillis were prepared for Sunday morning breakfasts occasionally, but always for New Year's Eve. Look below for their secret.

PALILLIS

3 cups all-purpose flour
3 teaspoons baking powder
1 teaspoon salt
3 tablespoons shortening
heated, canned, evaporated milk (1 cup or more)
Wesson oil or shortening
powdered sugar
honey

Sift flour, baking powder, salt. Using a pastry blender or fingers, work the shortening into the flour mixture until it is like coarse meal. Add enough warmed, canned milk to bring the dough to a soft consistency. You may need to add from 1 to 1 1/2 cups of milk. Knead until smooth - about 3 minutes.

Allow the dough to rest for an hour. Divide the dough into quarters. Roll out one quarter of the dough at a time on a floured board until it is a little less than 1/4 inch thick. Cut into 4-inch triangles.

Heat the oil or shortening in a tall 1 1/2 quart saucepan or deep frying kettle. When the oil is hot, almost smoking, fry one triangle at a time. Quickly spoon hot oil continuously over the palilli. The rush of hot fat will make the dough puff up into a cloud. If you do not spoon the hot oil over the dough, some palillis will puff and some will not, so the secret to success is to keep spooning the hot oil and fry the palilli until it is golden. Remove with a slotted spoon and drain on paper towels. Continue to fry and roll out the rest of the dough. This recipe may be divided in half, but children seem to have a huge capacity for these puffs. Serve them hot and sprinkled with powdered sugar. Some people like to poke a hole in them and dribble in a little honey as is the custom in New Mexico. Palillis must be eaten when they are hot and fresh as they are not good left over. Makes two dozen.

A picnic in the country.

CHAPTER VI

PICNICS

t the heart of all Early California dining was a love of picnics or tertulias, the dearest of all the eating ceremonies. To gather up whatever food and wine you could find and carry it off to the hills or woods to dine al fresco was considered a marvelous diversion.

One could think of a picnic on the spur of the moment or plan it days in advance to celebrate an honorable occasion such as the saint's day of a favorite señora or señorita. If it still was the nineteenth century, you would have ridden a horse to the chosen spot. Traditionally, the gentleman's sweetheart rode on his saddle, before him, like a captured princess. Trailing along behind came the dueñas complaining about the dust and flies as they bounced in the crude carts drawn by oxen.

Grandpa regaled us with the tales of his boyhood picnics when they would ride to a nearby spring, chosen not only for its charm, but also because dueñas could not follow in the carts. The picnic riders jostled one another off their saddles so as to steal a pasear and a flirt with as many girls as possible. As they leaped from horse to horse, the animals seemed to appreciate the fun as much as anyone and all would laughingly arrive at the picnic spot.

Luckily, there were always two or three more serious fellows to begin a fire and cut branches, paring them into skewers for the meat which would be threaded onto the green sticks and quickly barbequed. When the meat was ready it would be pulled off the stick with a tortilla to be folded at the bottom and sides and eaten immediately without plate or fork. The picnickers brought only the meat, the tortillas and the wine.

Like the picnic above, for me a true picnic must be somewhat natural, somewhat wild, enjoyed in a soft, green place with only rocks and stumps for furniture. For the table, a cloth or exotic carpet, far removed from a road or a bandstand or crowds. A true picnic is private and will give you a lovely feeling that you invented picnics. But your repast must be contrived enough so you have delightful things to eat, striking some wonder in the eaters. Meat laced onto a green stick and seared quickly over a flame is that kind of food. But I have known a sandwich tied up with an old Christmas ribbon to strike equal wonder in my guests, so perhaps surprise is as important as the picnic morsels themselves.

Just such a surprise did Grandpa create when Grandmama forgot the silverware for our lunch one afternoon. He took us searching in the nearby thicket for sticks. Soon he was at work with his pocket knife, paring a set of eight twig forks that to my delight we used to eat our potato salad.

Below is Grandmama's potato salad - not the midwestern farm version, redolent of boiled eggs, sweet pickles and mustardy mayonnaise - but her lighter version with its secret, always to douse the warm potatoes with plenty of wine vinegar.

GRANDMAMA'S POTATO SALAD WITH PARSLEY

12 new potatoes
 (but Russet will do if that's all you have)
1/4 cup wine vinegar
2 tablespoons fragrant olive oil
 mixed with 3/4 cup mayonnaise
1/2 cup parsley, minced
 (Grandmama used Italian parsley)
2 shallots or green onions, minced
1/2 cup black olives

Boil the potatoes in their jackets until done - 30 to 45 minutes depending on their size. Poke them with a small, sharp knife to test. If the potatoes are tiny and quite young, I sometimes do not peel them. This makes it easier to cut them into chunks and get them into a bowl while they are warm so they may be bathed with the vinegar. Allow the potatoes to marinate in the vinegar for at least 1 hour at room temperature. Taste and if they seem bland, sprinkle with a tablespoon or more of vinegar. Next, add the mayonnaise, parsley and olives, the shallots or onions. This potato salad is best eaten immediately while still fresh.

Mama's chicken was much better than Grandmama's, especially for toting to picnics. It was never oily, as fried chicken can often be, and was wonderfully spicy. One of the culinary rules of an Early California kitchen was to always rub or mash fresh garlic with salt in a mortar to remove the sharp bite before adding it to a dish. Mama, very much the inventor, just added more herbs and spices to the garlic paste and rubbed it on her chicken, pork chops and steaks.

MAMA'S SPICY CHICKEN

1 or 2 chickens, cut into pieces
1 lemon

Seasoning Paste:

5 cloves garlic
4 tablespoons sea salt
2 tablespoons paprika
1 teaspoon marjoram
2 teaspoons japones (small red peppers) crushed

Rub chickens with cut lemon being sure you squeeze juice under the skin. (Whenever Mama prepared Pollo con Arroz or Paella she also used an herb paste to rub on the chicken. See Chapter V.) Place all ingredients of the seasoning paste in a mortar and mash until well blended. Rub generously over chicken. You will need only a portion of the seasoning; store the rest of the paste in a jar in the refrigerator. Bake in 350 degree oven for 45 minutes. Next, place chicken under a hot broiler and sear for about 15 minutes, turning so the skin becomes crisp and turns a mahogany color. You may also place the chicken on a hot barbeque for 15 minutes, turning the pieces every couple of minutes. I sometimes add fresh, minced cilantro to the seasoning paste.

Even though Grandpa was a family man with five children he dressed like a dandy in pinstripes, linen shirts and straw hats. He owned a fashionable haberdashery while his brothers concerned themselves with the daily running of the ranch. After a hard day, Grandpa considered it to be his unchallenged right to stop off at the saloon when he felt the need for a whisky and water and a chat with his many cronies. Following this refreshment, he would buy an oyster loaf from the bartender to take home as an offering to Grandmama. Grandmama loved these loaves with a passion, but for her their memory will always be inextricably linked to saloons.

One day Grandmama decided to modernize by having a telephone installed. Aunt Alice phoned immediately with the news that Grandpa was at the saloon with another woman. When Grandpa came through the back door with the oyster loaf she accused him of infidelity. He calmly asked from where she had obtained the information and when she pointed to the new telephone Grandpa ripped the newfangled instrument off the wall, loudly proclaiming: "If that's what you use it for, you won't have it." Needless to say, Grandmama had the telephone reinstalled several weeks later and the "other woman" was never again mentioned. And Grandpa's whisky stops, complete with oyster loaf contributions, continued with regularity.

After the days when these delicious peace offerings could be purchased over saloon bars were long gone, Grandmama would hunger for them and learned to make them herself. They were frequently prepared for picnics as they travel well, with the flavors melding together, but they are most tempting just hot from the oven.

OYSTER LOAF

1 long loaf of crusty, French bread
a heap of oysters
butter
1 egg, beaten with 1 tablespoon of water
2 cups soda crackers mashed to fine crumbs
fine pepper
oil

Cut the loaf in half lengthwise and scoop out the insides, leaving a shell. Reserve the crumbs for another use. Brush the bread shells with melted butter and heat the loaves in the oven for about 5 to 10 minutes until toasty warm. Meanwhile, dip the oysters in the egg and water, letting all excess liquid drip off. Roll the oysters in the cracker meal and saute them in a mixture of butter and oil. Sprinkle with fine pepper. They should be golden, but not overcooked. When all the oysters are fried, heap them into the bottom bread shell, place on the top, press together and bake on a cookie sheet at 350 degrees for 15 minutes to heat the whole loaf through. Remove and eat immediately, or wrap in brown paper and tie with a string to carry to your picnic, the only needed accompaniment – a glass of chilled, white wine.

A very traditional picnic food was the albondigon or meat roll, almost a Spanish pâté, which was served cold along with sarsa and chunks of bread.

ALBÓNDIGON OR MEAT ROLL

1 chicken breast, boned and skinned

2 - 3 chorizos (be careful they are not fatty)

OR   1 pound homemade chorizo

2 pounds ground sirloin

1 onion

1 jalapeño (use more peppers for more picante flavor)

2 teaspoons chile powder

1 teaspoon garlic salt

1/2 teaspoon freshly ground pepper

1 teaspoon oregano

2 eggs, beaten

1 cup pitted, ripe olives, chopped

2 carrots, cooked and sliced lengthwise into thin pieces

4 tablespoons finely grated Parmesan cheese

1/4 cup heaped with chopped parsley

1 clove garlic

3 hard-boiled eggs

2 bay leaves

1 sprig fresh oregano

      OR   2 teaspoons dried oregano

1 can beef broth

water

Grind chicken breast in meat grinder or food processor. Do not overprocess. Chop onion finely. Mix together the ground chicken, onion, chorizo sausage, eggs, ground sirloin, jalapeño chile, chile powder, garlic salt, pepper and oregano. Blend well with your hands. Divide meat mixture in half and lay out two long rectangles of cheesecloth, wrung out in cold water. The cheesecloth should be of double thickness. Pat out the meat 1/4 inch thick, forming two meat rectangles approximately 8 inches x 12 inches. Sprinkle each rectangle with half the olives, Parmesan cheese, minced garlic, parsley, sliced carrots and the eggs which have been cut lengthwise into quarters.

Gently roll up the meat, using the cheesecloth to nudge it along. As you roll the meat, pat and form it with your hands to make sure the roll is tight. Tie string at both ends of the rolls. Place the two meat rolls side by side in a deep roasting pan. Add the bay leaves and oregano sprigs and cover with 2 to 3 inches of cold water. Cover pan tightly with foil and bake the loaves for 1 hour and 15 minutes, turning the loaves every half hour. At the end of the cooking period, life the rolls from the pan with wide spatulas and cool completely before removing cheesecloth. As the meat cools, it will firm up. It is best to make the albóndigones the day before you need them, as the flavor is at its peak when they have been chilled. The sliced albóndigon will be a mosaic of colors. Garnish with cilantro.

The Spanish rancheros surrounded their ranches with nopal cactus as thick and forbidding fences. The fruit of the cactus, the prickly pear or tuna, and the nopalito were both eaten and enjoyed widely. Nopalitos, the cactus leaves, are now available from time to time in markets. Buy only the smallest and thinnest joints of light green for they will be the most tender and are really worth the trouble. I was once served a salad of the most tender string beans I had ever savored – that turned out to be cactus leaves cut into julienne strips to resemble string beans. A salad of nopalitos is a perfect accompaniment to albondigon.

ENSALADA DE NOPALITOS

1 1/2 - 2 pounds nopalitos (small cactus leaves)

  OR   substitute canned nopalitos finos al natural

3 - 4 tablespoons olive oil

2 tablespoons vinegar

1/2 small white onion

salt to taste

fresh cilantro, minced

1 - 2 minced jalapeños en escabeche

  OR   jalapeños that have been seared and peeled

Scrape off the stubs of the spines left on the cactus leaf as if you were scraping a carrot. You do not have to peel off the thin, outer layer of green skin although the skin on older, large joints can be tough. Julienne the nopalitos so they resemble tiny string beans. Steam or boil in a couple inches of water, just until tender, about 10 minutes. Do not overcook or the nopalitos will release an inordinate amount of a jelly-like substance. IMMEDIATELY drain the nopalitos in a colander placed in the sink under a faucet of cold, running water. You must rinse off the sticky substance clinging to the cactus. It is a good idea to also rinse off canned nopalitos in the same way.

Toss the warm nopalitos with the olive oil, vinegar, salt, minced onion, Jalapeños and cilantro. You may toss in a few cubes of sharp Cheddar cheese or crumble some Mexican queso fresco over the top.

Grandmama was given many good recipes by an Italian friend who was an excellent cook. Her artichokes were incomparable and went with just about anything you would care to take on a picnic.

PIAZZA'S ROMAN ARTICHOKES

6 artichokes

1 lemon

2 cloves garlic, minced

1/4 cup minced parsley

1 teaspoon fresh mint, minced

1 teaspoon sweet basil, minced

1/4 teaspoon rosemary

1/4 teaspoon sage

1 teaspoon salt

1/4 teaspoon freshly ground black pepper

1 1/2 cup bread crumbs

> *(preferably made from stale, but not dry, French bread)*

1/4 cup olive oil

2 tablespoons Parmesan or Romano, freshly grated

1 egg plus a couple of tablespoons of artichoke liquid

Trim off the stems of artichokes and cut off the sharp points of the leaves. Open leaves and rinse well. Rub all cut surfaces with lemon. Boil the artichokes in a couple inches of water to which you have added 1 tablespoon of olive oil and the juice of the lemon. Cook for about 35 - 45 minutes, testing for doneness by pulling a leaf from the bottom. If done, the leaf will come off easily. Drain the artichokes upside down. For filling, mix the bread crumbs with the herbs, salt and pepper, 2 tablespoons olive oil, the cheese, egg and enough artichoke liquid or milk to make a moist stuffing that holds together. Pack a little of the stuffing between all the artichoke leaves and place in an oiled casserole. Bake uncovered for 25 minutes at 350 degrees. When Grandmama could not obtain fresh artichokes, she would pack this same stuffing in a pan with canned artichoke hearts and bake in a moderate oven for about 25 minutes. Cut into squares to serve.

MINIATURE ARTICHOKE FRITTATAS

Artichokes were grown on the ranch and one of our favorite ways of preparing them was borrowed from the idea of the flat Italian omelet, the frittata. We made tiny frittatas, quickly sizzled in hot olive oil. These can be served as appetizers, for a light lunch or to accompany you on your picnic.

4 artichokes

1 lemon

2 cloves garlic, minced

2 - 3 tablespoons parsley, minced

4 eggs, beaten

4 slices bread, preferably French
      soaked in milk and squeezed dry

1/4 cup Parmesan cheese, finely grated

3 leaves fresh sweet basil. snipped
        OR   1/2 teaspoon dry basil
1/4 teaspoon salt
freshly ground pepper
olive oil or basil oil (see Note below)

Remove sharp tips of artichokes by snipping with scissors. Cut off the bottom stem to level the artichoke. Bring one inch of water to boil in a large pot and add the artichokes, squeezing the lemon over them and adding the rind to the pot. Simmer for about 40 minutes or until a bottom leaf pulls off easily. Cool the artichokes until they are easily handled. Pull off all the tough leaves and reserve for nibbling. Remove the pale, center leaves and cut off the tender parts, placing in a mixing bowl. When you get to the heart, scoop out the fuzzy interior. Cut the heart into slices and chop roughly. Add to the bowl. Repeat the procedure with the rest of the artichokes. (If you do not have fresh artichokes, use 4 - 6 canned or frozen, unmarinated, artichoke hearts.) Add the garlic, parsley, eggs, soaked bread which has been well-crumbled, the cheese, the basil and the seasonings. Blend well.

Heat a couple of tablespoons olive or basil oil in a skillet on medium heat. Drop large spoonfuls of the artichoke mixture into the hot oil, flattening the frittatas with the back of a spoon. Cook about four frittatas at a time, until golden on both sides (about 1 minute on each side). Drain on paper towels. These are delightful for picnics as they are still tasty when cooled. This recipe is easily halved, but six people will easily gobble up the whole thing.

174

Note: Basil oil is a perfect way to reap the benefits of a large basil crop or is handy to make if you have discovered a market carrying fresh basil in season. Place 3/4 cup olive oil and 1 cup of clean, fresh basil leaves in a blender or food processor and grind into a paste. You may store large amounts of this basil oil in your freezer and remove a scoop of it for use in tomato sauces, marinara sauces, vegetable sauces, or use in sauteing – such as with the artichoke frittatas above.

Below is a recipe for all those nibblers who adore picante finger food and for those who can take their salsa by the jugfull. Jalapeño carrots are good on picnics, tailgates, inelegant cocktail parties and barbeques. Myself – I eat them every day with a piece of cheese and a glass of peasant wine. If I miss a day without them, I double up the next day.

JALAPEÑO CARROTS

2 bunches of carrots

1 cup white vinegar

1/2 cup cold-pressed oil (like safflower)

1/2 cup olive oil

1 white onion, sliced thinly

5 canned jalapeño peppers, seeds removed

1 teaspoon sugar

Buy the freshest, most tender, young carrots you can find. Remove tops and peel. Cut diagonally into 3-inch pieces. If the carrots are tiny, don't cut them - leave them whole. Using a steamer basket or a pot with a steamer insert, steam carrots for 6 minutes. The secret is not to overcook them as they must remain crisp; the cooking time is dependent on the size of your carrots.

Stir the sugar into the vinegar then add the rest of the ingredients. You may cut down on the number of peppers if you are bothered by picante flavors. Place the steamed carrots while hot into the cold marinade. Refrigerate. The carrots get better and better the longer they remain in the marinade, but if you can't resist, try one after a couple of hours.

ONION EGGS FOR PICNICS AND EASTER

Before the days of storebought packages of Easter egg coloring, mothers dyed Easter eggs with anything from coffee grounds to beets. We know an old California family, our own, who overlooks the artificial pink and green eggs and every year produces natural terra cotta eggs from their big pots of onion skin dye. These eggs seem to even taste better and we make them all year just to bring on picnics.

Onion Skin Dye:

Make friends with the man in the vegetable department of your grocery store and ask him to save you the skins he removes each day from the golden onions. You will need enough skins to fill up your large pot halfway. Add 2 yellow onions (skins intact) - cut into pieces - to the pot. The night before you wish to cook the eggs, place the onion skins and onions in the pot and cover with water. Add 1 tablespoon salt. Simmer for 1 hour and then turn off the heat and allow it all to steep overnight. In the morning you will have a pot full of flavorful, dark orange dye. Place 12 - 14 white eggs into the pot of onion dye and bring to a gentle boil. Boil for 5 minutes. Turn off the heat and let the eggs steep for another 10 minutes. If the eggs are not to be used for an Easter egg hunt or display, lift them out of the pot using a small strainer after the initial 5 minutes of boiling. Crack them all over with a table knife. Do not worry, the whites will be set. Place the well-cracked eggs back into the pot and simmer for another 10 minutes so they will absorb some of the onion flavor and, if you have done an admirable job of cracking, the eggs will be streaked with terra cotta onion dye.

If you want the eggs themselves, without the shells, to be colored, peel and place them to steep in some of the COOLED onion dye so they may color without overcooking.

These eggs are so beautiful, you will never make Easter eggs any other way.

TURKEY – WILD RICE SALAD

You will enjoy the varying textures of this unusual salad as it is a refreshing change from the traditional macaroni picnic fare.

1/2 turkey breast
2 tablespoons butter
1/4 cup water
1/2 cup white wine
1/2 cup wild rice
3 1/2 cups hot water
1/2 teaspoon salt
1/2 cup long-grain white rice
1 cup hot water
1/2 teaspoon salt
4 green onions (scallions) minced
1 1/2 cups tiny, young peas
1/4 cup toasted almonds, chopped

Vinaigrette Dressing:

1/4 cup wine vinegar
1 - 2 tablespoons fresh lemon juice
about 2/3 cup oil
1/2 teaspoon salt
2 teaspoons FRESH ginger root, minced finely

Blend the dressing ingredients together and set aside. Brown the turkey breast in the butter. Add the water and wine to the pot and cover tightly. Place in a 350 degree oven for approximately 1 hour and 20 minutes or until meat thermometer reads 170 degrees. Cool. Remove breast bone and cut turkey into cubes.

While the turkey is cooking, steam the white rice for 30 minutes. Leave lid on and allow the rice to steam off the heat for another 15 minutes. Place in a bowl, fluffing with a fork. Simmer the wild rice in the 3 1/2 cups water for 40 minutes or until tender. Stir frequently. Drain the wild rice and add to the white rice. Cook the tiny peas for 2 minutes or just until thawed. Stir in the scallions, peas, almonds and the diced turkey breast. Blend in the vinaigrette, taste for seasoning and add salt, pepper or lemon juice, as needed.

These velvety potato pan rolls were so good, Grandmama didn't need to bake any other bread except, of course, flour tortillas.

For picnics, we would fill the buttered rolls with good ham or chicken and watercress.

GRANDMAMA'S POTATO PAN ROLLS

1 stick butter, room temperature

3 tablespoons + 1 teaspoon sugar

2 teaspoons salt

2 well-beaten eggs

1 cup lukewarm, mashed potatoes

1 package of yeast

1 1/2 cups potato water

7 cups flour

1 egg

1 tablespoon water

poppy seeds (optional)

To yield enough potato water, you will have to boil two medium potatoes (cut into pieces) in 2 cups water for about 30 minutes or until tender when pierced with a knife. Drain off the potato water and reserve. Put one potato through a ricer or mash, adding potato water to make a creamy consistency. You should have 1 cup mashed potatoes. Reserve the other potato for another use. Stir the butter into the potatoes and cool to likewarm. Meanwhile, sprinkle the yeast over 1/2 cup of the reserved potato water. Stir in 1 teaspoon sugar. Proof for 10 minutes.

In large mixing bowl, blend the yeast mixture with 2 eggs, the salt, sugar, 1 cup potato water, and 3 cups all-purpose flour. Beat the mixture together until well blended. Next, add the 1 cup mashed potato–butter mixture. Slowly add 3 more cups of flour until you have a fairly stiff dough. Knead the dough for

8 - 10 minutes using the last cup of flour. If the dough seems sticky, allow it to rest 4 - 10 minutes. Add up to 1/2 cup more flour for kneading.

Place dough in a greased bowl to rise until doubled - about 1 to 1 1/2 hours. Punch down and place in refrigerator for 3 hours or overnight. Make sure the bowl is covered with plastic wrap and foil. Punch down the risen dough and form into 20 portions. Knead each portion on a floured board, then form into a smooth ball, tucking the sides under and pinching together.

Place the rolls, as you form them, on a greased baking sheet. They should be about 1 inch apart. Cover with a towel and allow them to rise for 30 - 40 minutes. Brush rolls with egg and water which you have blended together. Sprinkle with poppy seeds. Bake in preheated 375 degree oven for about 30 minutes.

Occasionally, when there were dried figs available, Mama would surprise us with filled cookies packed in an old tin. Otherwise, fresh fruit was the only dessert carried on picnics.

FILLED FIG BARS

1 1/4 cup butter

1/2 cup shortening

1 cup sugar

2 eggs

2 teaspoons vanilla

1/2 cup milk (sour)

> *OR   add 2 teaspoons lemon juice or vinegar to milk*

5 cups flour

1/4 teaspoon baking soda

2 teaspoons baking powder

1 teaspoon salt

Blend shortening, butter and sugar until creamy. Add eggs, vanilla and sour milk. Blend in flour which has been sifted with salt, baking powder and soda. Chill for 2 hours. Meanwhile, make the filling.

Divide the dough in half and roll it out, as you would for pie crust, into two sheets a little smaller than your cookie sheet. Roll dough between two pieces of waxed paper. Place dough on cookie sheet, spread with filling and cover with the other sheet of dough. Bake in moderately hot oven at 375 degrees for about 20 minutes or until slightly browned. Cut into strips while still warm. These cookies can also be shaped like turnovers.

Filling:

3 cups chopped dried figs

1/2 cup water

1/2 cup milk

1/2 cup sugar

1 cup pecans or walnuts, chopped

1 teaspoon grated lemon rind

1 tablespoon lemon juice

1 tablespoon butter

Grind figs with the sugar, using a food processor. Boil together the ingredients until the filling is juicy, yet thickened - about 10 - 15 minutes. Cool before using. Stir in nuts after filling has cooked and cooled.

Remember that even the simplest of foods taste wonderful under a tree (or in a tree). You may spend all morning preparing foods for one picnic or you may bring only a loaf of bread, some fruit and a jug of nectar. When a child, I would spread peanut butter on crackers and my brother and I would eat them in the top of the old walnut tree by the kitchen. Never a more sumptuous picnic.

Grandpa and Grandmama on the stairway of Don Jose's adobe.

CHAPTER VII

WEST COAST SEAFOOD

ummer or winter, there was a season for every prey and my mother's family took great pleasure in foraging nature's bounty, whether it be from the nearby shallow waters of San Francisco Bay, Half Moon Bay, the Diablo Mountains, the fields of Santa Clara Valley or the pristine streams of the Santa Cruz Mountains. They loved the hunt, something my quiet, German father shunned along with the raucous camaraderie which accompanied plucking mussels from rocks or netting crawdads. All of the seafoods (and river crawfish) included in this chapter are a part of the indigenous California cuisine which is now being newly recognized – alas, at a time when these foods are not so abundant.

My father, loving work more than play, also loved quiet almost as much as work. Anticipating the quiet of the redwoods, he and Mama bought some mountain property with grapevines and an apple orchard on a small river. The deer ate the grapes, someone stole the apples, and when springtime arrived, my uncles found out that the river was loaded with crawdads. We were inundated by uncles bearing makeshift nets and large pots with cousins and hungry aunts looking for a warm place to bask in the sun until lunch was ready.

It takes about 8 - 10 crawdads to make one person happy so you must have an energetic bunch of scavengers to crawdad if you are feeding a large group. The boiled crawdad has a delicate, sweet, lobster-like flavor. The pile of crawdad shells at the end of the lazy Sunday would do justice to any respectable Indian midden and my father was complimented at least a dozen times on his wise choice of riverfront property.

SAN LORENZO CRAWDAD BOIL

60 live crawdads

    OR   obtain frozen crawfish

large pot

assortment of spices:

    japones pepper pods, mustard seeds, bay leaves, sprig of oregano, thyme, crushed peppercorns

8-inch square of cloth cut from an old towel or sheet

string

The best time of year to crawdad is April or May. Choose a clean, unpolluted freshwater stream or river. Soak the crawdads in cold, salted water. Then wash the crawdads in several changes of water until the water is no longer muddy. The cooking vessel should be half full of boiling water in readiness. Tie up your chosen spices in the cloth and drop into the pot along with the salt. Drop in the crawdads, one at a time, cooking about 10 crawdads in each batch. Boil 5 - 10 minutes in the uncovered pot or until the crawdads turn red. Remove with tongs and add the next batch. When all of the crawdads have been cooked, pile 8 to 10 on each person's plate. Eat only the meaty tails. You may suck on the rest of the parts to extract bits of the prized, buttery fat. Most of the fat is found in the head. Pick it out and save for stock in cooking fish soups, ciopino or paella.

PACIFIC MUSSELS

Within the family fold, mussels were considered even more of a delicacy than crawdads – at least when crawdad season was over and mussel season was about to begin. On Sunday afternoons in November, we would journey to Half Moon Bay, finding the beaches cold and deserted.

We children were excluded from musseling. While the men were rolling up their pants they mumbled something about dangerous currents and we watched them longingly as they wandered toward surf-beaten rocks. Occasionally, we would turn from our sand castles to hear their shouted obscenities above the roar of the ocean. And then they would return, clutching at their tire irons and gunny sacks full of mussels. They would walk proudly like heroes to the warm campfires on the beach where their women waited with cups of coffee.

MUSSELING

Musseling does not have to be life-threatening. You can wade along the shore at low tide and look for the blue-black shells, clinging by their "whiskers" to rock walls. Pry them off their hold with a large screwdriver or a tire iron. Do not remove any mussel with an open shell, a sign that the mussel is dead. In California, it is safe to hunt mussels from November 1st through April. Mussels are highly toxic during warm months. If you are hunting in remote areas your good judgment will have to be your guide since quarantine signs are not posted everywhere during "off" months.

Preparation for Cooking:

If any of the mussels appear slightly open, squeeze them. If the mussel is alive he will quickly close his shell. If the mussel will not shut, throw it out. Place the mussels in a large bucket of seawater (or if you are at home use fresh water) and scrub off sand and algae with a stiff brush or pot scrubber. Grandpa would run his pocket knife around the mouth of the shells to remove the "beards."

On our musseling days, someone would have long since ordered the children to stack up beach driftwood and a few rocks would be set about strategically to keep the mussel pot off the coals.

Cooking of the Mussels:

Bring several inches of water to boil in the large mussel pot (a canning pot works well). Toss in 8 cloves of minced garlic, some parsley, a couple of teaspoons of thyme or oregano, 4 cups white wine, 4 cups water, and some freshly ground pepper. The mussels have plenty of natural salt. When the liquid is boiling, dump in about 6 quarts of well-cleaned mussels. A large pot will require 10 - 15 minutes of steaming, but a small pot of 2 - 3 quarts of mussels should be ready in 5 minutes. Keep checking the pot so that you can remove the mussels as soon as they open. Discard any mussels not open at the end of the cooking period.

By the time the pot of mussels is steaming over the campfire, the beach will be foggy and everyone will be gathered around the pot in their damp-smelling sweaters and wet trousers. Grandpa liked to impale loaves of sourdough bread on sticks and hold them over the coals until they were crackly and hot. Grandma's old porcelain tin plates would be handed around, heaped with mussels and a hunk of torn bread. Once the pot was emptied of mussels, the liquor at the bottom was poured into the plates of those who appreciated such delicacies and drunk thereof, adding at least another ten years to life expectancy we were told.

If you are steaming mussels at home, strain the broth through a clean dish towel to remove any sand (not a concern when eating on the beach) and reserve the broth for use in soups, chowders and rice dishes. Or drink it. A friend in San Louis Obispo likes to save enough mussels and broth to make a savory stuffing for roast turkey or chicken – the day after a mussel cook-out.

NORMA'S MUSSEL STUFFING

2 pints mussels, steamed
(or saved from the day before)
1 onion, minced
1/2 cup butter
1 teaspoon dried basil
OR 1 tablespoon fresh basil
1/2 cup parsley, minced
1 loaf French bread, stale
1 egg
reserved mussel broth, strained
3 1/2 pound chicken or 8 - 10 pound turkey
(double the above stuffing if you prepare a turkey)

Remove mussels from shells and chop roughly. After trimming crust from the French bread, cut it into cubes or grind it in a blender or food processor. Saute the onion in the butter until softened. In a bowl, assemble all of the ingredients, adding only enough mussel broth to moisten the stuffing but not make it soggy. Add more herbs, salt or freshly ground pepper to suit your taste.

STEAMED CLAMS

Great-grandma Cecilia was so fond of clamming she still insisted on trips to the mudflats of San Francisco Bay when she was ninety. Even during the twenties and thirties there were game wardens to make sure that only the limit of clams was gathered. However, Great-grandma excluded herself from such limits because she was taking as many clams as she wanted long before the game wardens were born.

During one morning of clamming, Great-grandma disappeared. Panic-stricken, everyone ran up and down the oozing mudflats, calling for her. After much yelling and scolding of the children for leaving her, the old lady appeared hobbling down the beach as though she had sprained an ankle. Everyone ran to help her. As they lifted her into the car, out dangled her black stockinged legs, covered with huge bulges. Her stockings held double her limit of clams but when her sons scolded her, she refused to discuss the matter, holding herself erect in the back seat as she was driven home to eat her clams.

Bentnose clams are usually dug in the morning so they can be taken home to soak in seawater with a handful of cornmeal. Place them in 1 gallon of cold water, 1/3 cup salt and 1/4 cup cornmeal. Change the water two or three times. By soaking in this solution, the clams will open and discharge the sand from their shells. After soaking, rinse the clams while scrubbing with a brush in running water.

Steaming:

Bring a couple of inches of water to boil in a large pot. Add the clams and steam until the shells open, about 4 to 5 minutes. You can pour a mixture of fresh lemon juice, melted butter, minced garlic and parsley over the opened clams.

FRESH ABALONE

In spite of the fact that, outside West Coast communities, abalone can be eaten only in the dried or canned state, it must be included here because it is one of the most special, indigenous foods of California. When the first Spanish explorers arrived they were offered a meal of abalone by the Coastal Indians.

Until the last ten years abalone was here for the taking in tidepools and found easily at minus tide along the shorelines.

The early rancheros, who enjoyed huge mid-morning repasts, often breakfasted on fried fish and abalone.

In dwindling abundance abalone can still be found off the California coast and adjacent islands. There are pink, green, red, black and the highly prized white abalone. It was the white abalone, taken from deep waters off Anacapa Island, which was obtained for me by my husband and a diving friend when we were to entertain the French cook, Simone Beck. We wanted to serve her something she had never eaten, so to accompany an elegant menu of layered omelets and fresh pear tarts, we had lightly sauteed white abalone, proclaimed by Simca to be as fine as milk-fed veal. Below is the recipe created for her.

ABALONE SAUTE

2 whole abalones
> *(do not use black abalone as it is best saved for chowder)*

several tablespoons sweet butter
3 tablespons mild onion or shallot, minced
juice from lime
1/2 teaspoon Dijon mustard
1/2 cup dry vermouth or white wine

Trim off the dark, tough edges of the abalone and discard or save for chowders. Slice the abalone into 3/8 inch slices or steaks, keeping as even as possible. You will need a razor sharp knife for this operation. Using a wooden tenderizing mallet,

192

pound around the edges of the steak and then once or twice in the center of the steak. It is not necessary to pound abalone into lacework. Only black abalone (the type frequently found in shallower waters) needs this heavy treatment. Pound lightly around the steak a second time. After the light pounding, the abalone will noticeably relax. You should have from 8 - 10 steaks.

Heat 3 tablespoons of butter in the saute pan until foamy. Add the minced onion, sauteing for a couple of minutes and then place 2 or 3 abalone steaks in the pan. Saute for about 30 seconds on each side. Remove and keep adding a tablespoon more of butter and when foamy, add more abalone. When you have sauteed all of the abalone, set it aside to keep warm and pour in the wine, lime juice and Dijon mustard, scraping up the browned bits. Reduce the liquid a little and then pour it over the abalone, attempting to glaze all of the steaks with some of the sauce. Serve immediately with warm bread or noodles. Fresh abalone is available seasonally in California fish markets and in Oriental markets.

ABALONE RICE

This cold salad, obviously good for picnics, occurred to me one summer on our sailboat when I had both leftover rice and leftover abalone done in the manner described above.

3 - 4 leftover abalone steaks, cooked and cubed
2 cups leftover white or brown rice

2 ribs of celery, sliced thinly

1/4 cup minced onion or shallots

3 tablespoons fresh lemon juice or white wine vinegar

1 - 2 teaspoons Dijon mustard

1/2 cup mayonnaise

1 tablespoon minced parsley

strips of canned pimiento

If you do not have leftover rice, place 2 cups water and 1/2 teaspoon salt to boil. Add 1 cup white rice and return to boil. Place on a tight-fitting lid and steam on low heat for 30 minutes. Turn off heat and let rice steam for another 10 minutes. Do not remove lid. Cool before using for rice salad. Place 2 cups rice in a bowl and fluff with a fork. Blend the lemon juice and mustard into the mayonnaise. Stir the onion, celery, the seasoned mayonnaise and the parsley into the rice. Add the abalone cubes. Taste for seasoning. Garnish with strips of pimiento.

ABALONE STUFFED WITH DUXELLES AND SHRIMP

In this recipe I veer from my California background and use duxelles, a rich mushroom paste used to season many French dishes, to fill abalone steaks. These particular duxelles, inspired by Simca Beck, are good combined with rice, minced ham, baby peas and then stuffed into anything from squab to fish.

DUXELLES

1 pound sliced mushrooms
1 cup canned, evaporated milk
freshly ground pepper and nutmeg to taste
salt to taste
3/4 cup cooked shrimp

Saute the sliced mushrooms in a nonstick skillet until they begin to release their juices, about 5 minutes, then douse them with the milk and simmer until they are creamy and thickened. Add a couple teaspoons of lemon juice. Season to your taste. Place in a food processor and finely chop. Do not puree. Stir in the shrimp. Set aside while you prepare the abalone. This duxelle filling is also good spread onto filets of Dover sole, rolled up and baked with a little butter and wine. Bake at 350 degrees for 18 - 20 minutes or until fish flakes.

Preparing abalone and sauce:

8 abalone steaks (about 1 1/2 pounds), lightly pounded
4 - 6 tablespoons butter
2 tablespoons flour
1 cup milk
1/2 cup clam juice, bottled
2 tablespoons sherry

Melt about 2 tablespoons butter in a saute pan. Saute 2 - 3 abalone steaks 30 seconds on each side. Remove and saute the other steaks in the same way, adding a little butter to the pan each time. Set the steaks aside, keeping warm. Stir the rest of the butter into the pan juices, adding the flour. Cook the roux for 2 minutes without browning. Add the milk, clam juice and sherry. Simmer the sauce over low heat, whisking, for at least 8 minutes. Lay out the abalone steaks and spread with the duxelle-shrimp mixture. Fold the sides of the steaks toward the center. Place seam side down in a long, buttered, heat-proof dish. Cover the abalone with the warm sauce and place under a hot broiler until the sauce is glazed and golden. Garnish each abalone roll with a shrimp. Usually each person can eat two of these rolls.

POACHED SALMON WITH AVOCADO SAUCE

Fresh salmon becomes available in fish markets in early spring and lasts until the end of summer. Its delicate flavor should be treated with respect and to my mind, poaching is one of the most respectable methods.

4 salmon steaks, 6 - 7 ounces each
3 tablespoons butter
1 cup dry, white wine
about 1 cup water
1/4 cup chopped onion

Melt the butter in a high-sided, twelve-inch saute pan. When the butter is hot, add the salmon. Saute 1 minute on each side. Douse with the wine and water. Add the onion to the liquid. If the salmon is not covered with liquid, add more water. Bring to a gentle bubble, turn the heat down to low and poach for about 7 more minutes (without lid). Test with a fork – you want it to flake. Remove the salmon to a serving platter and cover to keep warm. Reduce the remaining liquid by half over a medium heat. Meanwhile, start your sauce.

Avocado Sauce:

2 tablespoons butter
1 1/2 tablespoons flour
1/2 cup hot milk
1/2 cup salmon broth
3 tablespoons fresh lemon juice
dash hot pepper sauce
1 ripe avocado, sliced
salt and freshly ground white pepper to taste
3 tablespoons chives, snipped

Melt butter in saucepan. Stir in flour, cooking the roux for 2 minutes without browning. Add the hot milk and 1/2 cup of salmon broth. Simmer the sauce for 5 minutes, whisking until smooth. When thickened like a light cream, pour the sauce into a blender. Add the avocado, lemon juice, salt, pepper and hot pepper sauce and puree to a lovely green. Pour the sauce over the salmon steaks, sprinkle with chives and garnish with cherry tomatoes.

SQUID OR CALAMARI

Up to now, this stepchild of the more glamorous shellfish has been appreciated by certain ethnic groups or those wise eaters who have harbored a well-kept secret - that squid is one of the most delicious of the mollusks.

Squid is now being flash-frozen and is increasingly available throughout the country. Also marketed now are squid steaks, similar to pounded abalone. In many cases, squid, known in California as the poor man's abalone, can substitute for abalone and conch (available off the Florida coast and in the Caribbean), to which it is very similar in taste and texture.

After you first clean this maligned shellfish and you end up with its milky white meat, the subsequent cleanings will not be difficult.

Cleaning Squid:

First, separate the head from the body by simply pulling. Using a sharp knife, trim off the tentacles or arms, just below the eyes. Discard the head. Reaching inside the body of the squid, pull out the inedible quill. Pull off the little fins and peel off the purplish, translucent membrane which covers the body. The pearly, white surface will now be revealed. Do not leave on the membrane as it tends to be tough. Use running water and your finger to dislodge any of the gelatin-like white deposits inside the cavity of the squid. If you do not plan on stuffing the whole squid, cut it open along the side so that you may clean out the deposits more easily. For stuffing, leave the body whole. Otherwise, cut the squid into rings, strips or squares.

SQUID AND ONION RINGS IN BEER BATTER

The cardinal rule with both squid and abalone is: DO NOT OVERCOOK. The following beer batter is light and airy and quickly cooks to a golden color before the squid can toughen. This batter is also wonderful with zucchini sticks and onion rings. If you heat the oil properly to almost smoking, 375 degrees, the coating will be crisp and never greasy.

Beer Batter:

1 1/2 cups all-purpose flour
1 can beer
oil or melted shortening
1 pound squid (approximately)
    cleaned and cut into rings

Blend flour and beer together in a large bowl. Cover with plastic wrap and let the batter rest for at least 3 hours at room temperature.

Meanwhile, prepare the squid and dry well with paper towels. When batter is properly rested, heat at least 2 inches of oil in a deep frying pan or electric skillet. When almost smoking, dip a piece of squid into the batter, letting the excess drip off. Drop in the hot oil. Turn once. Lift out with a small strainer and place to drain on paper towels. You can fry several squid rings at a time once you get into the pattern.

If you wish to cook zucchini sticks, blot away all moisture with paper towels, dip in batter and fry quickly as with the squid. If preparing onions - remove skins, leaving the outside layer of the onion intact. Cut into 1/4 inch slices. Separate into rings. Dip in batter, letting excess drip off. Fry in the hot oil, turning once. Drain on paper towels. To keep them warm until you finish frying, place the onion rings on a baking sheet in a 200 degree oven. Zucchini sticks do not keep as well, tending to become limp. This is enough batter for about 3 large onions or 8 zucchini or a couple of pounds of squid.

CALAMARI SALAD INSPIRED IN BERKELEY

Of all the numerous ways to serve squid, one of our favorites is the calamari salad, inspired by a friend in Berkeley, a gastronomically knowing town that provides shelter for many squid eaters. This salad is perfect for picnics or summer lunches when you want to cater to appreciative palates.

1 1/2 pounds squid, cleaned and cut into strips

reserved tentacles, chopped roughly

1 pound medium shrimp

2 cans beer

1 pound mussels or clams

   (see pages 186-191 for preparation)

Lemon Dressing:

2 tablespoons white wine or sherry vinegar

1/3 cup fresh lemon juice

2 cloves garlic mashed with 1/2 teaspoon salt

2/3 cup olive oil

1/2 teaspoon marjoram

2 tablespoons parsley, minced

1 tablespoon cilantro, minced

   (optional, but we love it)

1/2 cup pitted black olives

freshly ground black pepper

Vegetables:

2 carrots, scraped and cut into long slices

1 green pepper, cut into strips

   (if I have the time I sear the peppers over a flame
   and peel off the thin skin)

1 red bell pepper cut into strips (optional)

Place the squid in a 3 quart saucepan and pour boiling water over it. Cover with a tight-fitting lid and allow the squid to steep for 1 minute. Check to see if it has turned solid white. When it is pinched it should feel tender. If not, let it poach in the hot water a little longer but keep checking. Drain and set aside while you prepare the other seafood.

Simmer the shrimp in hot beer until it turns pink, but no longer than 2 - 5 minutes. Shell and devein and add to the squid.

Prepare the clams or mussels. Steam in a couple of inches of hot water for 4 - 6 minutes or until they open. Discard any closed shells at the end of the cooking period. Add the clams or mussels (in their shells) to the above seafood.

Prepare the dressing. Toss with the olives, the seafood and the vegetables. Taste for seasoning. This salad is best eaten shortly after preparation.

BARBEQUED RED SNAPPER

The Pacific Red Snapper is available throughout the year, is inexpensive, and its firm flesh is perfect for grilling over coals.

3 1/2 - 4 pound whole red snapper or rock cod

3 cloves garlic

1 teaspoon salt

1/4 cup olive oil

5 leaves of fresh sweet basil

    or 1 1/2 teaspoons of dry basil

1 lemon

hinged grill

Place the garlic, salt, oil and herbs into a food processor or blender and puree. Slash three diagonal cuts through the skin and flesh of the fish on both sides. Rub the herb mixture into the cuts generously. Squeeze lemon juice into the cavity of the fish and rub a little of the herb mixture inside. Rub vegetable oil inside the hinged grill to prevent the fish from sticking. Place the fish inside the grill and set over whitened coals. Do not place fish directly on a barbeque rack. (Hinged barbeque grills are indispensable in cooking whole fish and butterflied fish, as well as fish steaks and filets over outdoor fires.) Grill about 20 – 25 minutes, turning twice. The herbs and garlic penetrate the fish and the slashes help the fish cook evenly.

For Friday fish nights and some of the days preceding Lent, Grandmama could be relied upon to cook one of her favorites - codfish croquetas. She took great joy in shopping in the Italian and Portuguese markets of San Jose, where baccala or the necessary dried codfish could always be found. Search for boneless salt cod, but if you cannot find it, you can remove the bones after the initial cooking. Fresh cod is not an adequate substitute for the special flavor of dried cod.

GRANDMAMA'S CODFISH CROQUETAS

1 pound salt cod

1 cup mashed potatoes (cooked without salt)

2 tablespoons onion, finely minced

3 tablespoons butter

1/4 teaspoon cayenne pepper

4 tablespoons parsley, minced

2 egg yolks

about 1/2 cup vegetable oil

1 1/2 cups stale bread crumbs
  (preferably from French bread)

Soak the salt cod overnight in cold water. Remove from soaking water and rinse under running water. Put in a large pot and cover with cold water. Bring to a simmer. Simmer gently for 15 - 20 minutes or until tender. Remove and cool. Flake the fish and remove all of the bones. Place the flaked fish in a bowl with the rest of the ingredients (except the oil and breadcrumbs). Mix well with a wooden spoon or your hands. Chill for easier handling. Grandmama liked to form the codfish mixture into finger-shaped croquettes. Roll the croquetas in bread crumbs. Heat the oil in a heavy skillet. Saute the croquetas until golden on both sides. They can be eaten as an appetizer, for luncheon or a light dinner. Serves 4 - 6.

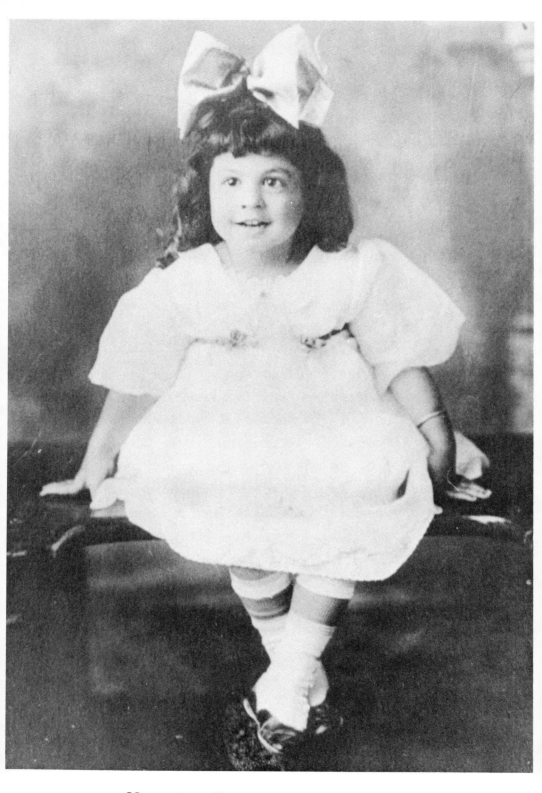

Mama, at age five, as sweet as angel pudding.

CHAPTER VIII

SWEETS

esserts in the early days were a rarity among the rancho foods because of the scarcity of sugar, which had to be shipped from Boston or Mexico. The Californios contented themselves with an after-dinner glass of sweet wine or angélica. A platter of fresh fruit such as grapes, apples, pears or peaches was usually offered, with each guest served a little knife with which to pare his own fruit. If romantically inclined, a gentleman would offer to peel an apple for his lady. Later, when sugar was no longer an exotic luxury item, fruit still remained the favored dessert unless someone brought an imported box of chocolates or candies.

Mama had a touch (unequaled in the family) for desserts. She was taught the art of pastry making by Aunt Nicolassa who, in spite of the fact that she had been blind since the age of sixteen, cooked all the meals for her brothers living on the ranch. Grandmama's pies were leaden so we would eat the sweet fillings and, when she wasn't looking, spirit out the crust under a hat or napkin and give it to the chickens. But as for Mama's pastry she could never make enough.

When apricots were at their peak Uncle John would send for the young Marie (Mama) and it was understood that she would make him all the pies he desired. Quite a task. It was necessary to make at least four pies at a time as Uncle John would eat one pie at each sitting. Not only was her pastry exquisite but the ripe, dark orange apricots from the ranch orchard were ambrosia.

MAMA'S APRICOT PIE TO FEED ONE UNCLE
(or six ordinary people)

Pastry:

2 cups all-purpose flour

1/2 teaspoon salt

2 teaspoons sugar

1 stick butter

4 tablespoons shortening

1 cup of water, well-chilled with 4 ice cubes

   (you will need about 3 - 4 tablespoons of ice water)

Place all dry ingredients in a bowl. Add the butter cut into pieces, and the shortening. Using the tips of your fingers or a pastry blender, blend the shortening and butter into the flour until it is mealy. Continue working until there is no unblended flour left. Add the ice water in small amounts, preferably 1 tablespoon at a time. Try not to add more than 4 tablespoons of water. The less water you need to add, the better. The dough must be just damp enough to hold it together, but not so damp it is sticky. Place the dough on a floured board. Using the heel of your hand push the dough several inches across the board. You will be layering the butter in the pastry. Push the dough at least three times. Pat into a flat 8-inch circle. Wrap in plastic wrap and chill for 2 hours.

Apricot filling for 9 inch pie:

4 cups ripe apricots, sliced in half and pitted
     or use canned apricots in natural fruit juice
     (rather than heavy syrup)
1/2 cup sugar
1/2 cup brown sugar
3 teaspoons quick-cooking tapioca
1 tablespoon lemon juice
1/2 teaspoon almond flavoring

Preheat your oven to 400 degrees. Prepare the apricots and place in a bowl with the rest of the ingredients. Toss until the fruit is well-coated.

Line a 9-inch pie pan with half the pastry, reserving half for the top. Fill with the apricots. Roll out the rest of the dough and place on top of the fruit. Seal and crimp the edges. Cut at least four slits in the top crust. Bake at 400 degrees for 10 minutes. Reduce heat to 350 degrees and continue to bake for 35 minutes or until crust is golden brown.

When winter came and Mama could not make her juicy fruit pies filled with raspberries, boysenberries, apricots or peaches she turned to lemons and again we could not decide which pie we liked best because her incredible lemon pies were the best lemon pies any of us ever tasted.

MAMA'S INCREDIBLE LEMON PIE

For your crust, follow the pastry recipe given for apricot pie, chilling the dough for 2 hours.

Lemon Filling:

5 tablespoons cornstarch

2 tablespoons flour

1 1/4 cups sugar

1 2/3 cups milk

1/3 cup lemon juice

4 egg yolks, slightly beaten
    (save whites for the meringue)

2 teaspoons finely grated lemon rind

2 tablespoons butter

After preparing pastry (according to preceding recipe) and chilling, roll out 2/3 of the dough (reserve the rest for another use) and fit into a 9-inch pie pan. Grease a piece of foil and place on top of the pastry, pressing against the sides. Weight with dry beans. Bake in 400 degree oven for 15 minutes. Remove foil and beans and prick any puffy spots. Return to oven, which you have turned down to 375 degrees. Bake pastry shell for 15 more minutes or until golden. Cool before filling.

In the top of a double boiler, mix the sugar, the flour, and a little of the milk into a smooth paste. Add the rest of the milk and cook over simmering water for 10 - 15 minutes, stirring constantly. I like to use both a whisk and a spoon, alternating. The whisk blends away lumps and the spoon reaches into corners. The pudding should be thick enough that you can draw the whisk over its surface, leaving traces. Beat a tablespoon of the hot pudding into the egg yolks and then beat the yolks into the pudding. Cook for 3 minutes longer. Add the lemon rind, juice and butter, blending well. Cool slightly before filling pie shell.

Meringue:

4 egg whites
1/4 teaspoon cream of tartar
6 tablespoons sugar
1/2 teaspoon vanilla

Whip the egg whites until foamy. Add the sugar 1 tablespoon at a time and continue to beat until the whites hold stiff peaks. Beat until no granules of sugar can be felt when meringue is rubbed between the fingers. Add the vanilla and spoon the meringue lightly over the lemon filling. It is important to bring it to the edge of the pastry crust so as to seal in the filling. Bake in a preheated 350 degree oven for about 12 minutes or until the tips of the meringue are golden.

To Use Your Extra Pastry:

Roll out the pastry scraps (after chilling) and cut into strips using a sharp knife or pastry wheel with decorative edges. Sprinkle with sugar and cinnamon or with Parmesan cheese. Bake for 15 - 20 minutes in a 350 degree oven.

WALNUT ORCHARD PIE WITH FRENCH PASTRY CRUST

The walnut harvest was always so abundant we tended to use walnuts lavishly in many desserts. Chocolate chip cookies were studded with as many nuts as they could bear to hold, cinnamon rolls were really walnut rolls. And then there was Mama's special walnut pie. In the autumn my brother and I would be pressed into hulling walnuts, leaving our hands black for a week. I, in particular, would be highly offended at the sight of my hands but my feelings could be assuaged by Mama's pie, custardy and light - unlike the usual nut pies which can be overly sweet.

Pastry for single 10-inch bottom crust:

1 1/3 cups all-purpose, unbleached flour

1 stick butter, chilled and cut into small pieces

2 teaspoons sugar

1/2 teaspoon salt

1 small egg

> *(if you use a large egg you will need only 3/4 egg)*

3 teaspoons cold milk

Place all the dry ingredients in a bowl. Add the chopped butter, working the fat into the flour by using a large fork or pastry blender until mealy. Beat the egg (or 3/4 egg) with the milk and sprinkle half of this liquid on the flour-butter mixture. Stir with a fork. Add the rest of the liquid by drops, making sure the dough does not become overly damp. Stir again with a fork. If you stick your fingers into the dough it should not feel sticky. Push the dough mass together with your fingers. Place the dough, barely clinging together, on a lightly floured board. Push across the board with the heel of your hand. Scrape up dough using a spatula or a pastry scraper. Push dough across the board again and scrape up again. This step layers the butter throughout the dough. Form into a round and chill for at least 20 minutes or wrap in plastic wrap and place in a plastic bag and freeze.

You will find this dough even flakier after freezing, so I usually make several batches at one time and keep it on hand. Thaw at room temperature for about 1 1/2 to 2 hours.

As an alternate method a food processor can be used to mince the butter into the flour with "on-and-off" starting and stopping. Add the liquid a little at a time with this procedure. DO NOT LET THE DOUGH FORM A BALL AROUND THE BLADE. When the dough is just clinging together dump it out of the processor and push it across the board with the heel of your hand as above described.

For a pie or tart roll out the dough and place in a 9 - 10 inch baking tin. Chill while you prepare the filling. Note: This filling is deep so be sure you have pressed the pastry well against the sides of the tin to create high sides.

Walnut Filling:

1/2 cup brown sugar

3 eggs

1/2 cup sweet cream

1 scant cup light corn syrup

2 teaspoons vanilla

1 cup chopped walnuts

8 whole walnuts for garnish

Beat eggs well. Add the brown sugar, cream, corn syrup and vanilla. Stir in the chopped nuts. Pour the filling into the unbaked pastry crust and arrange the whole walnuts around the edge of the pie. Place in a preheated 350 degree oven and bake for 55 minutes. Do not overbake as the filling will continue to set-up after the pie is removed from the oven.

When fruit was not eaten as an after-dinner treat it was frequently used to make the dessert itself. During the Christmas holidays Mama served trays of her creamy glazed apricots along with a variety of nuts.

CREAMY GLAZED APRICOTS

1 pound dried apricots
1 cup sugar
1/2 cup canned milk (important)
1 teaspoon vanilla

Simmer the sugar and milk in a saucepan until the sugar is dissolved and a sauce-like consistency is achieved (about 5 - 8 minutes). Remove from heat and stir in the vanilla. Stir the apricots into this milk syrup. Using a sharp fork lift the glazed apricots, one by one, out of the syrup and place on waxed paper to cool. When cool store in a covered container. The glaze will harden on the surface but will remain creamy inside which is what makes these apricots so delightful.

FLOATING APRICOT PUDDING

Speaking as a connoisseur of puddings I would call this the Queen of Puddings.

1 1/4 cup sugar
2 tablespoons water

3/4 cup chopped, dried apricots (packed)

1 1/4 cup water

4 eggs, separated

2 tablespoons sugar + 2 teaspoons cornstarch

1 1/4 cup milk

1/2 teaspoon vanilla

5-cup metal ring mold

Caramelize the 3/4 cup sugar and 2 tablespoons water in a heavy saucepan over medium heat. Once the sugar begins to melt, swirl the pan frequently over the heat. Do not stir the sugar. After the sugar turns liquid, watch it carefully – it should be a golden caramel color – not dark brown. Pour the caramel quickly into the ring mold, tilting to cover sides of the mold. Be careful as the mold will be hot.

Cook apricots in 1 and 1/4 cups water until tender – about 15 minutes. Remove from heat and let cool after draining. Beat egg whites until stiff (reserve yolks) then add the 1/2 cup sugar by the tablespoonful. Gently fold in apricots and spoon into mold. Place mold in a water bath (a roasting pan with two inches of hot water works well). Bake in preheated oven at 350 degrees for 45 minutes or until done. If it browns too quickly, cover the top of the meringue lightly with a piece of foil and finish baking. To test insert a toothpick to see if meringue is set. It will rise in the manner of a souffle. Remove from oven and cool before running a knife around the edges. Place a serving platter on top of the mold and reverse in order to release the meringue.

While meringue is baking, make custard sauce by stirring the egg yolks with the 2 tablespoons sugar and cornstarch over medium heat. Add milk and stir constantly until custard thickens to sauce consistency. Do not allow the custard to come to a boil or it may curdle. Remove from heat and stir in vanilla. Cool, then pour sauce over meringue and allow to chill for several hours or overnight. Serve six - delicately.

Puddings and custards in all of their guises were popular desserts but the one we grown-up children remember is *jericalla*, so light and airy it was aptly named angel pudding. *"Jericalla, jericalla, come, y calla,"* chanted the children. "Pudding, pudding, be quiet and eat."

When my brother and I were small we would find occasion to feign illness, knowing full well that Grandmama would rush over with a huge bowl of angel pudding, akin to custard and clouds. It is simple to prepare for a sick child who needs sustenance or for an adult who wishes he were a sick child.

ANGEL PUDDING

4 large eggs, separated

1 cup sugar

1/2 cup flour

> *(I sometimes use 1/4 cup cornstarch in place of the 1/2 cup flour)*

1 quart whole milk

2 teaspoons pure vanilla

cinnamon

In saucepan beat yolks until light and slowly add sugar and flour. Heat milk in separate pan until hot. Slowly whisk hot milk into egg mixture and cook over medium heat until thickened. Remove from heat and add vanilla. Beat egg whites until they stand in peaks and fold lightly into the warm pudding. Sprinkle the top with cinnamon. It is very comforting to sit in bed eating a bowl of warm angel pudding.

The following recipe was given to me by a good friend who lives in a rambling, adobe house high above the Mojave Desert and who, in this setting, creates ethereal desserts. This flan will be like velvet upon the tongue if you follow the deceptively simple directions and cook it ONLY until a light film of custard clings to a knife plunged gently into the flan's middle.

SPANISH FLAN

1 cup sugar
aluminum 2 quart mold or flan pan

---

6 egg yolks
2 eggs
2 large cans evaporated milk
3/4 cups sugar
2 teaspoons pure vanilla (Mexican Papantla)

Baño de Maria

216

Caramelize the sugar by swirling it in a saucepan over medium heat. Do not stir. When it is liquid and light brown, remove from heat and pour quickly into a 2-quart round mold. Quickly circulate the pan to cover sides with caramel. Work fast; it hardens quickly.

Beat egg yolks, eggs, milk and sugar together until blended but not too frothy. Add vanilla. (Variation: Add 1 tablespoon grated orange peel + 2 tablespoons orange juice in place of vanilla.)

Pour egg - milk mixture into caramelized pan. Use flan pan lid or aluminum foil to cover pan tightly. Place in large pan like a roaster filled with at least 2 inches of hot water. (Baño de Maria.) Bake on the lowest rack of oven preheated to 350 degrees for approximately 1 hour and 5 minutes. The flan will continue to cook after you remove it from the oven.

Test for doneness: Using a sharp knife insert blade 1 inch from edge of pan. Knife should be clean with no custard clinging to it. When you insert the knife into the center of flan there should be a film of custard, not large curds, clinging to the knife. Do not insert knife all the way to the bottom of the mold or the top or your flan will have a scar. After cooking chill flan in its mold for several hours or overnight. Before unmolding run a sharp knife completely around the edges of the flan. Move the pan from side to side to see if the flan is slipping and free of the pan. Place a flat serving platter with edges on top of the mold and reverse. The flan should slip easily onto the platter with the caramel sauce on top and

217

around the edges. Cut the flan in wedges, spooning a little more caramel sauce over each heavenly piece. Serve preferably at room temperature.

Many custards, puddings and cakes soaked in spirits are found among the most popular of Californian and Mexican desserts because they are a welcoming cool finale to the typical spicy meal.

Trifle was popular on the ranch once staples like sugar and jams could be found in the pantry. They especially liked to add spirits to any dessert and leftover cake and pudding became one of their favorites. The sponge cake recipe given below will make 2 8-inch cakes or 1 large 9 1/2-inch cake baked in a springform pan.

SPANISH TRIFLE

Trifle ingredients:

1 8 or 9-inch sponge cake (recipe below)
OR day-old pound cake
1/3 cup raspberry jam (preferably seedless)
OR apricot jam
1/4 cup dessert sherry or brandy
2 cups of leftover angel pudding (page 216)

Sponge cake:

5 whole eggs

1 cup sugar

1 cup + 1 tablespoon cake flour

1/4 cup cornstarch

2 tablespoons milk, room temperature

1/2 teaspoon vanilla

1 teaspoon grated lemon or orange rind

Preheat oven to 375 degrees. Grease pans (or springform pan) and line with waxed paper or parchment, being sure to also grease the paper. Place the eggs and sugar in a metal bowl (preferably the one that goes with your electric mixer) and whisk until well blended. Place the bowl over simmering water and continue to whisk constantly, about half a minute, until the mixture is warm. Your whisk must move constantly so the eggs do not coagulate. Now place the bowl under your electric mixer or transfer to the proper mixer bowl and beat at high speed, using the whisk attachment, about 10 minutes or until the mixture has tripled in volume and cooled. Remove the bowl from the mixer. Place the cake flour and cornstarch together in a sifter. Sift 1/3 of the flour - cornstarch over the egg mixture and fold using a wide spatula. Continue to sift and fold until you have gently added all of the flour - cornstarch. Do not add the liquid until there is no trace of flour. Stir together the milk, vanilla and lemon peel and fold into the cake batter using as few strokes as possible. Place the pans into the preheated oven and bake for 20 - 30 minutes, depending on the size of your pans. The cakes should be a light golden color and

219

spring back when pressed. Cool in the pans for 5 minutes and then remove by turning upside down on cake racks. I use one 8-inch cake for trifle, reserving the other cake for another time. These cakes freeze beautifully.

Assembling trifle:

Simmer the jam and the sherry together until just warm and well blended. Slice the cake in half and place in a pretty bowl with 3-inch high sides. If your cake is more than a day old cut it into cubes so more surface area will be covered with jam and pudding. If you are using an attractive glass or crystal bowl, line the sides with sliced strawberries or use canned fruit such as apricots, cherries and mandarin oranges. Spread the cake with half of the jam and pour half of the pudding over the top, making sure it runs down the sides and goes under the bottom. Place the next half of the cake on top and add the rest of the sherry, jam and pudding. Decorate with more of the strawberries or whatever fruit you are using. Cover tightly with plastic wrap and refrigerate a couple of hours before serving.

Before concluding this lengthy subject of puddings you must have the recipe for rice cream - the concoction all Latin mothers stir up for a family dessert. Not only are they fond of puddings but they love rice almost as much as frijoles. Even though rice cream is "everyday" soothing it can be found in the most fashionable restaurants of Mexico City. Obviously, those who have dined well still look for the comfort of a good rice cream.

CREMA DE ARROZ

(Rice Cream)

1 1/2 cups boiling water
2 tablespoons butter
1/2 cup long-grain rice
3 cups whole milk
2 egg yolks
> *(3 egg yolks for a richer consistency)*
1 cinnamon stick
1 2-inch piece of vanilla bean
1/2 cup to 2/3 cup sugar
1 teaspoon vanilla
cinnamon

Combine the water and rice in a saucepan. Bring to a boil and cook for 15 minutes. Heat the milk, sugar, vanilla bean, and cinnamon stick in the top of a double boiler. Add the steamed rice to the milk. Simmer uncovered for 45 minutes in the double boiler. From time to time stir around the edges of the pan where the milk coagulates. After 45 minutes, the rice will have absorbed a third or half of the milk. Remove the double boiler from the heat. Now place the rice - milk directly over medium heat, stirring constantly until the milk begins to resemble cream (about 10 minutes). Next beat a spoonful of the hot rice cream into the yolks and pour the yolks (back) into the pudding.   Stir over the heat for 2 minutes or until thickened. Remove from heat and cool slightly before pouring into a shallow bowl and sprinkling with cinnamon for serving.

MANGO MOUSSE

The exotic quality of this dessert would have astounded Los Californios of old with their bowlsful of figs and glasses of angélica, and yet it is a luxurious, cool ending to a highly seasoned meal. If you want a less rich dessert make the amaretto crust another time and just enjoy the mousse with its hint of fragrant mangoes and orange.

3/4 cups mango pulp, fresh or canned
*   (you may substitute with stewed, dried apricots;*
*   drain off excess liquid before pureeing)*
1 teaspoon grated orange peel
1 envelope plain gelatin
1/2 cup orange juice
1/4 cup Grand Marnier
1 cup pastry cream (recipe follows)
1 cup whipping cream
4 egg whites
*   (you will have these left after making pastry cream)*
2 tablespoons sugar
1/4 cup toasted, slivered almonds for garnish

Blend mango to a puree using a blender or food processor. If you use canned mango drain off excess liquid. Add orange peel. Set aside while you soften the gelatin in the orange juice by placing it in a metal measuring cup and setting in a little pan of hot water, stirring until gelatin dissolves. Combine mango puree, the Grand Marnier, the gelatin mixture and the pastry cream (which you have made earlier and cooled). Set aside while you whip 1 cup of heavy cream until light. Whip the egg whites into soft peaks. Add the 2 tablespoons sugar and whip until stiff but not dry. Blend the whipped cream into the mango - custard mixture and lightly fold in the whites.

You may place the mousse in crystal wine glasses, small dishes or a springform pan with amaretto crust. Before serving sprinkle with toasted almonds.

AMARETTO CRUST

1 cup plain vanilla wafers
1/2 cup Italian amaretto cookies (both crushed finely)
1/2 stick butter, melted

Blend together. Press into bottom and sides of an 8 or 9-inch springform pan. Bake for 8 minutes at 350 degrees. Cool. Fill with mousse.

PASTRY CREAM

1 cup milk

1/4 cup sugar

2 tablespoons all-purpose flour

4 egg yolks (reserve whites for mousse)

1 tablespoon butter

1 teaspoon vanilla

Blend flour and sugar together in top of double boiler, slowly adding milk. Simmer for about 8 minutes or until mixture has sufficiently thickened. Add some of the hot mixture to the yolks and then blend the yolks into the hot pudding. Stir together constantly for about 4 minutes until thick. Remove from heat, add the vanilla, and pour into a bowl, rubbing the butter over the top of the pudding to keep a skin from forming. Chill before using.

PINEAPPLE CREAM PIE

This is a memory from Mexico where the pineapple was always in ample supply, so very sweet and never too acidy. We spent many delightful hours sitting in our sunny patio eating chunks of it with the warm juice rolling down our arms while we tried to think of all the various ways to use this exquisite fruit.

Crust:

10 graham crackers, finely ground
10 vanilla wafers, finely ground
3/4 stick of butter, softened
10-inch Pyrex pie plate

Blend crumbs and butter and press into the pie plate. Bake at 350 degrees for 8 minutes. While crust cools prepare:

Filling:

1 cup fresh pineapple, shredded
2 tablespoons sugar
8 ounces cream cheese, softened
1 cup crema doble
> (the day before stir 2 tablespoons buttermilk into 1 cup whipping cream; leave in a warm spot until thickened - about 8 hours; refrigerate and it will thicken more)

1 cup sugar
3 eggs
1/2 cup blanched almonds, toasted and ground
1 cup sour cream
1 tablespoon powdered sugar
1 teaspoon vanilla

Shred pineapple in food processor. Combine with sugar and cook over moderate heat until juice has evaporated. Cool. Blend cream cheese, crema doble and sugar until smooth; then add eggs, almonds and vanilla. Stir the cooled pineapple into the cheese mixture and pour into the crust. Bake in a preheated 350 degree oven for 30 minutes or until set. In a bowl combine the sour cream, sugar and vanilla and spread over the top of the pie. Place back in the oven for 3 more minutes. Remove and chill overnight covered with plastic wrap.

MAMA AND BRER RABBIT'S BEST GINGERBREAD

Mama made the highest and lightest gingerbread I have ever tasted. It belongs to cold, winter evenings when just the smell of these spices baking makes the world seem less lonely. Mama played with all of her recipes, including this one which was originally inspired by a bottle of Brer Rabbit molasses in 1940.

1/2 cup butter, softened

1/2 cup sugar

2 eggs

2 cups all-purpose, unbleached flour

1/2 cup whole wheat flour

1 1/2 teaspoons baking soda

1 teaspoon cinnamon

3/4 teaspoon ground ginger

1/2 teaspoon cloves, powdered

1/2 teaspoon salt

1 cup molasses

1 cup hot water

2 teaspoons vanilla

Cream butter and sugar. Add the eggs one at a time. Sift all dry ingredients together. Combine molasses and hot water, blending well. Add the dry ingredients to the egg - sugar mixture alternately with the liquid ending with the flour mixture. Beat after each addition. Add vanilla. Pour into a 9 x 9 x 2-inch pan and bake at 350 degrees for 45 minutes.

BANANA FRITTERS

Fritters were a popular dessert on the ranch because there was so much fruit available. Living in Mexico we became especially addicted to banana fritters which in our family force all other fritters to take a back seat. Attesting to our addiction to bananas is our custom of baking whole bananas in their skins, then slitting them open to sprinkle with brown sugar and cinnamon. We often ate these hot bananas for breakfast in Mexico on our blue-glazed terra cotta plates, and if we were lucky we had some of the thick cream from San Juan del Río to pour over the fruit.

This batter is also delicious with pineapple rings or fresh apricots that have been halved. You may use dried apricots if they have been lightly steamed and drained. Fruit should be dusted with flour so the batter will stick. These fritters are especially good for breakfast and, if made with canned pineapple rings, they make an excellent side dish with ham or roast pork.

6 firm bananas, peeled and halved lengthwise

1 cup all-purpose flour

2 teaspoons baking powder

1 teaspoon salt

1/4 cup sugar

1/3 cup milk

    (sometimes a touch more)

1 egg

1 teaspoon vanilla

1 tablespoon vegetable oil

oil for frying

Sift the dry ingredients together. Place 1/3 cup milk in measuring cup, add 1 egg, the vanilla and vegetable oil. Beat together and add to the dry ingredients stirring just until blended. You may have to add more milk if the batter is too thick. The oil for frying should be heating in a pan or use an electric fry pan. Dip each banana half in batter and fry until golden. Drain on paper towels, sprinkle with sugar and cinnamon and serve while warm. The banana, because it's fried, softens to a pudding-like consistency and yet the fritters will remain crisp even after slightly cooled.

ANISE COOKIES WITH WALNUTS

These are crisp cookies meant for dipping in wine, coffee or hot chocolate. They will keep for weeks stored in a tin.

1 3/4 sticks butter (7 ounces)

1 cup sugar

1 cup brown sugar

3 tablespoons anise seeds

5 tablespoons brandy

2 teaspoons vanilla

6 eggs

5 1/4 cups unsifted flour

3 teaspoons baking soda

2 cups finely chopped walnuts

Grease four loaf pans and set aside. Mix sugar, brown sugar and butter until creamy. Add the anise seeds, brandy, vanilla and eggs, beating in the eggs one at a time. Sift the flour and baking soda together. Slowly stir the flour into the batter. Add the nuts. Spoon the batter evenly into the pans. Bake at 350 degrees for 45 - 50 minutes or until a cake tester inserted in the middle comes out clean. Cool for 10 minutes and remove the loaves from the pans. Using a serrated or sharp knife, cut the loaf into 1/2 inch slices. Lay out the slices on baking sheets. Return to a 375 degree over for 8 - 10 minutes. Turn the slices and toast for another 5 - 10 minutes or until golden. Cool the cookie slices and store in tightly covered containers. They will keep for several weeks.

PRUNE CONSERVE

My mother, known as Sister in her large family, was one of the best cooks around. When fruit was being harvested in the rancho orchards, her uncles would clamor for her pies and she would bake dozens each week while the fruit lasted.

When the prunes came Mama, Grandmama and Aunt Nicolassa would put up prune jam that contained lots of raisins and walnuts. It is divine spread over freshly baked bread like the potato rolls on page 180. Whenever they made jam they always made the bread too because the two delights were expected by all to appear together.

Mama kept a notebook, all shaggy and worn with use, containing all her recipes. Years after she was gone, I searched and searched through her book for the prune jam recipe, but none was to be found. When my husband was courting me his mother gave me toast and homemade prune jam for breakfast one lovely morning and - wonder of wonders - there was Mama's jam. Now my husband claims I married him for a jam recipe.

Below is a treasured "receipt" from the Grimmett family.

ONE PLUMP HUSBAND'S GREAT AUNT ANNA'S PRUNE OR PLUM CONSERVE

4 cups plums or prunes
>   *(if using dried prunes cut them into quarters and soak in hot water for one hour and drain)*

1/2 cup orange juice

3 cups sugar

3/4 cup raisins

1 cup broken walnut meats

3 tablespoons brandy (optional)

Put plums, which have been pitted, through the medium blade of a food chopper or chop in a food processor. Combine the chopped fruit, the orange juice and the sugar in cooking pot. Allow the fruit and sugar to steep for 1 hour. Add the raisins and simmer on low heat until thickened. Depending on the type of plums, the thickening will take anywhere from 10 - 15 minutes. Stir in the walnut meats and the optional brandy. Pour into hot sterilized jars and seal immediately or seal with paraffin. Makes approximately three 8 ounce jars.

CANDIED FIGS

We had bountiful crops of figs and candied them so they'd be preserved to enjoy all year.

5 pounds fresh figs (Black Mission or any available)

1 pound granulated sugar

1 cup water

Wash and drain the figs. Place in a large pot with sugar and water and cook slowly for 1 hour, covered. Remove from heat and let stand overnight. The second day boil for 1 hour with the cover off. Let stand overnight. On the third day, again boil slowly with cover off until the figs are almost dry or syrup has almost completely boiled away.

Place on a platter or waxed paper and dry in the sun. Or, if that is difficult or the weather won't cooperate, place them to dry in a gas oven as the pilot light heat will dry them slowly. This process will take a couple of days. At the ranch they were always sun-dried, but brought in late in the day before the evening dew came in from the Bay. The figs must be turned occasionally. You can judge when they are dry enough for your taste.

It is not absolutely necessary but the figs can be rolled in granulated sugar before being placed in tight cans or jars. Flatten them as you pack for storage.

On the ranch someone had planted a peach tree on the very edge of the adobe's veranda to eliminate the long walk to the orchard for a peach. Dried plums or prunes – as with the dried apricots and figs – saw us through the long winter when we could not pluck a peach from the nearby tree.

Since Mama took complete charge of the pastry making and cake department, it's any wonder that Grandmama ever bothered, but she made a moist prune cake that was loved by everyone. It is the old-fashioned cousin to the ubiquitous carrot cake of today.

GRANDMAMA'S PRUNE CAKE

1/2 cup butter, room temperature

1 cup sugar

1/2 cup brown sugar

2 eggs

2 cups hot prunes

2 tablespoons prune juice

1/2 cup buttermilk

1 teaspoon grated orange rind

1 1/2 cups all-purpose flour

1/4 teaspoon salt

1 1/2 teaspoons baking powder

1 teaspoon baking soda

2 tablespoons bitter cocoa powder

2 teaspoons cinnamon

1/2 teaspoon cloves

1/2 teaspoon nutmeg

1/2 teaspoon allspice

1 cup chopped nuts

1 cup raisins steeped in 2 tablespoons hot sherry

To prepare the prunes steam them in 1/2 cup water for 10 minutes. Drain and reserve liquid. Chop prunes. Cream the butter and sugar until fluffy. Add the unbeaten eggs one at a time, beating well after each addition. Sift together all dry ingredients and set aside. Add the prunes and 2 tablespoons prune juice to the creamed mixture, then stir in the dry ingredients, nuts and raisins. Pour into a greased 12-cup bundt pan and bake in a 350 degree oven for 35 minutes or until a toothpick inserted in the center comes out clean. Pour the following glaze over the cooked cake or simply sprinkle with powdered sugar. We think this cake is even better after being aged for a couple of days well wrapped in foil. Glaze it only when you are ready to serve it.

Glaze:

4 tablespoons softened butter
3/4 cup powdered sugar
1/4 cup cream, heated
1/2 teaspoon vanilla

Blend sugar and butter together until smooth. Whisk the warm cream and vanilla into the sugar mixture. If necessary add more cream.

VELVET HOT CHOCOLATE

Custardy, hot chocolate was much beloved in my family. It would make you think better and be stronger if you drank it very early in the morning. Then while the rest of the world went about sleepwalking the drinker of the chocolate would be vigorous and equal to all the chores of the day. Now we save Velvet Hot Chocolate for a special Sunday breakfast or for the same winter evenings that seem to require hot gingerbread.

4 squares semi-sweet chocolate, grated

1 cup boiling water

4 cups milk

1 cup cream

2 - 3 tablespoons sugar

1 teaspoon vanilla

1/2 teaspoon cinnamon

a pinch each of allspice and nutmeg

1 egg + 1 egg yolk, beaten

Boil the chocolate in the water until melted, stirring constantly. While you whisk, add the milk and the rest of the ingredients. Cook for 1/2 hour in the top of a double boiler. The chocolate will thicken so it will coat a spoon. After removing the chocolate from the pan, it is best to pour it into a high pitcher so you can properly beat it for several minutes with a whisk until it is very frothy. Serve velvet chocolate with hot, buttered toast or croissants and you will be in heaven.

The following recipe was given to me by an imposing old lady who grew up on a rancho, now long gone, near San Luis Obispo. She swears on the formula's efficacy and confided that it was given the name of that illustrious northern city because it was visitors from San Francisco who drank so much of this elixir when they came to spend holidays on her ranch. I give you the recipe precisely as she so kindly gave it to me.

PUNCH SAN FRANCISCO

Take a large, clean crock and when the first fruit of the season appears (the first fruit should be the dark, sweet cherries) pick enough to fill 1/3 of the crock. Cover them with a nice sherry. When the apricots are ripe take only those having a distinct perfume and layer them on top of the cherries and sherry. Cover the apricots (now filling 2/3 of the crock) with nice old brandy. At last, when you can get the perfect sweet peaches layer them into the crock and cover with some more of the nice old brandy. Now you must end it all with some champagne - only half a bottle or so - for you and your lover must drink the rest of the bottle.

Put the crock to rest in the cellar or some other cool spot until Christmas. Serve for the holidays, throwing out the fruit and hoping that not too many of your visitors are from San Francisco.

INDEX

UNUSUAL SPANISH WORDS AND EXPRESSIONS

The Spanish language within this book is used in a light-hearted fashion. By the twentieth century, only a few ancianos and scholars used the native tongue of the Californians in the pure sense. The Early Californian descendants as I have known them - my uncles, Grandmama, Grandpa, Mama, Godmothers and Aunts peppered their English conversations with some Spanish and idiomatic phrases. I have purposely excluded from this list, Anglicized words such as tortilla and hacienda.

abrazo	embrace
anciano	old man or old one
almuerzo	mid-morning breakfast
angélica	sweet dessert wine of Early California
arroz	rice
asador	the chief man in charge of barbecues
"Buen Provecho"	"Eat well," an expression used at the onset of a meal
carne asada	barbecued meat
carne seca	jerky or dried meat
chilaquiles	fried tortillas simmered in a casserole with cheese
chilena pie	corn and chicken pie
chile relleno	fresh chile stuffed with meat or cheese
chimichuri	refers to a green parsley sauce served with meat

cilantro	fresh coriander or Chinese parsley
cocido	stew
colache	vegetable stew of zucchini, tomatoes and corn
demonios	devils or demons
dueña	chaperon
epazote	an herb of unusual flavor, used in cooking beans; grows wild in some parts of the United States
fandango	a festivity with much dancing
flan	baked rich custard
frijoles de olla	beans cooked in an earthenware pot
frijoles refritos	mashed beans fried in oil or lard
gente de razón	the Spanish people of Early California as opposed to the natives or Indians
gran pipas	barrels of oak used to transport foods by ship
jericalla	soft boiled custard
las comidas del país	native foods
Los Californios	the people of Early California
masa	specially treated dried corn which has been blended to a meal and mixed with water; can be purchased at tortilla factories
masa harina	dehydrated masa not to be confused with cornmeal; can be purchased in supermarkets under the Quaker brand

merienda	late supper
migas	fried garlic bread
mole	refers to a classic sauce of chiles, spices, nuts and chocolate. There is a green mole made with husk tomatoes (tomatillos)
mostaza	field mustard greens which grow wild in California
nopalitos	cactus leaves
picadillo	a spicy mixture of ground meat, spices, and nuts
paisano	fellow countryman
palillis	fried pastry
pan relleno	stuffed loaf of bread
parilla	barbecue grill
puchero	stew
riata	lasso used by rancho cowboys
sarsa	another term used for tomato salsa
*salute**	a toast to fortune and good health
soldado de cuera	soldier
tertulia	picnic
tomatillo	green husk tomato
vaquero	cowboy

— NOTES —

— NOTES —

— NOTES —

— NOTES —

— NOTES —